Saved
(LaJuan Craig: Assassin Or Saint?)

GERALD C. ANDERSON, SR.

Editors:

Beryl Brackett

Andra Richardson, Lushe Consulting, LLC
www.lusheconsulting.com

Copyright © 2018 Lyfe Publishing

All rights reserved.

ISBN:0692196080
ISBN-13:9780692196083

Dedication

This novel is dedicated in loving memory to my sister, Arimentha Jackson (August 21, 1966 – April 13, 2018). You will be forever missed. May you rest in peace my love.

Prologue

Soon, she heard the pitter patter of feet running in her direction. She smiled. It was times like these she enjoyed. Behavioral analysts would liken her to a Hedonistic serial killer who is driven by the thrill, lust, sex or pleasure. But in LaJuan's case, it was about financial gain brought on by murder.

The footsteps drew closer to LaJuan, and she readied herself for the climax. He was now close enough. She stepped from behind the building and aimed at his head. She smiled, seeing the fear in his eyes, and pulled the trigger. He never had a chance to even beg.

One shot to the forehead was all it took. Don was dead before he hit the ground. LaJuan's mission was complete. She turned and walked down the sidewalk satisfied that she had taken this man out. After all, she despised him anyway. He was too cowardly.

***

Minutes after LaJuan left the scene, another car pulled up. A man jumped out of the vehicle and ran to the fallen body. First, he looked at the body with disbelief. A crowd was gathering, many of them mystified because the dead man looked exactly like the man standing over him. They had to be twins.

The man knelt down and hugged the corpse with all the strength he had. On the inside, he was boiling and knew that revenge was the name of the game. He was going to kill the person responsible for killing his brother. He didn't care how long it took; he was going to have his revenge.

1

Three years later...

LaJuan Craig was the world's greatest assassin, but only a few knew her real identity. She kept her circle small. Today was a day she could have used her best friend in the world. Raine Davis didn't know LaJuan thought of her as her best friend but to LaJuan, she was the best.

LaJuan regretted every bad thing she had done to Raine. Raine's spirit was true and forthright. She only wanted to be a star but had to pay a high price for that fame. LaJuan admired Raine because she got out of the organization—something no one else had achieved and lived to tell.

Today was the best day of LaJuan's life. She gave birth to a child and named her Kim. LaJuan didn't have many days where she smiled because she did something good. This was the first of those days on her short list. She was in love with Kyle, but she knew it couldn't last. If the men in suits found out about the baby and Kyle, their lives could be in danger. She couldn't tell anyone. She had to make Kyle understand that she couldn't be in his life or the baby's life.

The nurse brought in Kim, and LaJuan's face lit up like a Christmas tree. She had never been this excited in her life. Her first and only child was being handed to her for the first time. She would cherish this moment forever.

Kim looked up into her mother's eyes, and LaJuan wanted to cry. LaJuan said, "Baby, Momma can't be a part of your life, but I will see to it that you have everything you need. No one will bother you. I promise you a better life than I had." LaJuan continued to smile as her child seemed to be at ease in her arms. LaJuan had never known this joy.

She kept up with Raine as she had both of her children. LaJuan wanted to be there, but she knew Raine wouldn't allow it. She thought about calling to tell her the news. This time she even picked up the phone and dialed Raine's private number, but after one ring, she hung up. She didn't want to be disappointed. No one in LaJuan's life ever made her feel this way. She considered Raine to be the only sibling she had. Unfortunately, Raine had no love for her.

Kyle walked in smiling, "Hey, baby! How are my two beautiful ladies doing?"

LaJuan laughed, "We're fine and you?"

Kyle said, "Doing good."

LaJuan prepared herself to tell Kyle the bad news. She knew he wasn't going to take it well, but LaJuan had an assignment. She had to be in Spain in two days to assassinate a businessman who was making trouble for her organization. It was her job, after all. She knew if she didn't do it, the men in suits would come after her. She also knew she couldn't tell Kyle who or what she really was. If she did that, she would be lost to him forever.

LaJuan leaned back on the bed, "Kyle...I have to tell you something."

Kyle asked, "What is it, baby?"

LaJuan answered, "Well, I have to leave." She paused wondering what kind of response she would get. If the expression on Kyle's face was any sign, she knew it wasn't going to be good.

She continued, "My job is requiring me to go to Spain. I won't be back."

Kyle was visibly angry, "What do you mean you won't be back? You're not just going to up and leave. You just had a child—our child."

LaJuan explained, "I know, but my job is not the ordinary kind of job, Kyle. I have to go, and I don't have any choice. I'm leaving Kim with you. Please take care of my baby."

Kyle was in disbelief, "This is crazy! You can't do this to Kim or me. Your daughter won't even know you!"

"You don't think I've considered that?" LaJuan reached for a folder that was sitting on the table, "Here take this folder. Open it after I leave and follow the instructions to the letter. Please follow the instructions, Kyle. It could mean life or death for all three of us."

Kyle stood there, angry and in disbelief, "You are starting to scare me. What the Hell are you into, LaJuan? Has this been the real you all along?"

LaJuan looked down at Kim and then back up at Kyle, "Yes, but I can't get into it with you. Trust me, you're better off not knowing."

Kyle said sternly, "You're not going to do this to us!"

LaJuan didn't respond. There was nothing Kyle could do to stop it. She was going to complete her job, and that was all to it. She would never come back to him or Kim. She couldn't because the men in suits would use them against her. LaJuan knew better than anyone how the organization worked. She was willing to risk her own life, but for the first time, she wasn't willing to risk the lives of anyone else, especially Kyle and Kim.

***

A year and a half later...

LaJuan stood in the house across the street from Kyle's mother. Since her birth, Kyle had given Kim to his mother to help raise as LaJuan instructed. She knew Kim would be better off if she were somewhere not connected to her. LaJuan suspected the men in suits might know about Kyle, but they couldn't know about Kim.

She smiled endlessly as she watched her baby girl play in the plastic swimming pool her grandmother got for her. LaJuan wanted to take pictures, but she didn't want them traced back to Kim. She would have to capture the images in her mind and remember them forever.

LaJuan wasn't sure if Kyle told Kim about her. He was so angry when she left, but he just didn't realize that she had to do it. I think he suspected she was living a double life but to his credit, he never said anything.

She watched until Kim went inside. It was good because the neighbors were pulling up and LaJuan had to slip out the back door. No one would know she was there because she was too good to leave any trace of ever being there. The men in suits taught her that as well.

The drive to her appointment was a quiet one. She didn't want to listen to the news or music. The news depressed her because she knew the men in suits were behind most of it. The music always made her think of Raine. She really missed her friend, and she had to make a point of going to see her again even if Raine threw her out.

She pulled up in the back of the church. This was the last place LaJuan ever expected to be. Recent events made her give thought to trying to change her life.

Her meetings with Pastor Ponder usually lasted an hour, and they were productive. LaJuan was learning. She knew the demonic side of life, but she didn't really believe that God loved everyone. If her life was a testament, then He didn't.

She had gone through so much that she didn't think she was ever a child of God. Yet, every time she met with Pastor Ponder, he seemed to hit home. Then there was her daughter. She thought she could stay away easily, but that wasn't working either. She longed to hold Kim in her arms again. The images of her playing in the pool were on an endless loop in her mind. LaJuan felt the cold-hearted killer side of her slipping away.

She went inside the church and proceeded to the office. She thought, *"One of these Sundays, I'm going to actually attend a service. Then again, who am I really fooling?"*

She arrived at Pastor Ponder's office, "Hi, I'm Amy, and I'm here to see Pastor Ponder." LaJuan laughed inside knowing she didn't look anything like an "Amy," but she thought it was a cute name.

The secretary replied, "Go right in. He's expecting you."

LaJuan did as she was instructed. The Pastor was sitting at his desk working on his computer. He acknowledged LaJuan, and she could see he had an earpiece in and was talking on the phone.

She took a moment to get acquainted with her surroundings—something she always did when she went into a room no matter how many times she had been there. She had to know where everything was, and she had to have an exit plan. That was ingrained in her when she went through training.

Her training experience was tough on her because she was the only girl, and she was only 18 years old. The trainers made her work extra hard. LaJuan believed they didn't think she could make it through, but she proved them all wrong.

Once during an exercise, she failed to spot a knife on a table in the corner of a room. Her trainer took the knife and stabbed her in the thigh, causing her excruciating pain. They bandaged the wound and made her run a mile obstacle course on her wounded leg.

It was one of the worst experiences of her life, but it taught her to completely survey a room and to miss nothing. She had to know where everything was in case she needed to protect herself.

Pastor Ponder hung up from his call, got up, and hugged LaJuan. She didn't like the hugging, but she allowed it because he was a pastor. She figured he was safe.

Pastor Ponder said, "It's wonderful to see you again. To be honest, I didn't think you would come back."

LaJuan forced a smile, "I gave you my word. I keep my word no matter what."

"Did you think about what I told you last time?"

LaJuan forced another smile, "I did, and I still don't think God cares one bit about me. If I could tell you everything that I've been through, you would understand what I mean."

Pastor Ponder smacked his lips, "Miss Davis..."

"Please call me Amy."

Pastor Ponder continued, "Amy, God is the only one that truly cares for you. Until you tell me all that you have gone through, I can't really help you. This is a completely confidential atmosphere. No one will know what you tell me, and I would die before I divulge anything you share with me."

LaJuan laughed inside knowing that if the men in suits found out, they would surely put that statement to the test. She respected Pastor Ponder, but he had no real idea of the reality of the world. He might believe in God, but she's seen the devil.

"Pastor, I wish I could tell you my story, but I just don't know. I can tell you this—when I was a child I was raped multiple times by a man that was supposed to protect me. Two or three times a week he would sneak into my room and rape me. Where was God when this was happening to me?"

Pastor Ponder eyes were deeply saddened by LaJuan's word, "Honey, I can't tell you where God was then but the fact that you are sitting in this church, in my office, tells me that He's pulling at your shirttails, wanting you to come to him. Listen to the voice and take that step. We can take your confession right here."

LaJuan laughed outwardly, "No Pastor I don't think so. I'm nowhere near buying into this Jesus stuff."

Pastor Ponder said, "Then let's start with your life before the harshness started. Did you ever have a happy life?"

LaJuan thought about her life before her mother remarried. She started, "Yeah, there was a time when life was truly great. I was happy. I don't think about it much because it seems so distant."

Pastor Ponder said, "Tell me about it."

LaJuan was hesitant to say. She had never told anyone any part of her life, but now she was sitting in this pastor's office about to tell him what life was about when her dad was alive. She often wondered what she would be doing now if he had lived, but she knew she was destined to live the life she is currently living. She never had a chance.

She replied, "Well, when my dad was alive, life was great. We had a nice house in a nice neighborhood, and I went to a decent school. I would come home from school, and my daddy would be there. He would help me with my homework, give me a treat before my mom came home, and then he always took time to show me different things. He was an engineer, so he taught me a lot. When he died my life ended, and this one began."

Pastor Ponder asked, "It must have been tough for your mother also."

GERALD C. ANDERSON, SR.

LaJuan snickered, "My mom...she didn't care. I think she was shacking up with my stepfather before my dad died. Most women don't like having a good man. It's boring to them. They want a guy they have to worry about all the time. My mother never had to worry about my dad. He was a great father and husband, always home or at work, always paid the bills, and never cheated."

Pastor Ponder said, "You were a bit young to know all that weren't you?"

"I was, but I could tell he was hurting. Sure, he had nothing but true love for me, but when my mom came home, he changed. The pain was evident on his face."

Pastor Ponder responded, "That's sad. How did he die?"

LaJuan paused. It was a hard subject for her to talk about but she continued, "One day, my dad was driving home from the store. My stupid mom had him go to the store late one night. On the way home, he stopped to help someone whose car had broken down. It was a setup. When he went to help, they jumped him and beat him up. They could have just taken his money and left it at that, but they killed him."

Pastor Ponder said, "I'm sorry. I can see that's tough for you to talk about."

"It is, and when I became an adult, I looked into his death. It seems my mom and stepdad set him up. She sent him to the store on purpose, and my stepdad was the one who beat him up and killed him. I was glad I killed them both."

Pastor Ponder asked, "Do you know that for sure?"

LaJuan was confident, "Yes, I know it for sure. They did it for money—money they spent up in days. Before you knew it, we back in the projects because they spent all the life insurance left by my dad." LaJuan's phone rang, notifying her that she had a text. It was from the men in suits. She had another mission.

After reading the text, she said, "Well, Pastor, you know when duty calls, I have to go."

Pastor Ponder stood up, "Okay, young lady. I hope you will come back another time."

"Well Pastor, I wouldn't give up on me yet. Something may change."

Pastor Ponder said, "Oh I'm not giving up, young lady. Seeds are just being planted right now."

LaJuan was confused, "What does that mean?"

Pastor Ponder just smiled, and LaJuan stared for a moment, "Well bye, Pastor."

"Bye, young lady."

LaJuan left the office and headed to her car behind the church. Her mission was in South Africa this time, so she had to be on a plane in two hours. The life of an assassin never ended.

***

Pastor Ponder's secretary smiled as LaJuan walked out of the room. She quickly picked up the phone and dialed a number, "This is Chanel, code XJT553."

The voice on the other end said, "Thank you. Hold on."

Another voice came on the line, "You have information for us?"

Chanel answered, "She was just here for a second meeting with the pastor. It lasted only a few minutes, and she didn't say anything about your organization. She only talked about her childhood."

The second voice replied, "Thank you. That will be all."

The line went dead, and Chanel breathed a sigh of relief.

2

It was Raine Davis' biggest day ever. She prepared for her pre-release party at the Forum in Inglewood, California. She didn't know that LaJuan would be in attendance. For the last five years, LaJuan watched Raine. She would attend any concert she could, and she wouldn't miss this one for the world. The men in suits got her good seats but away from Raine's view. She didn't want her best friend to see her there.

LaJuan stood in the lobby waiting to go into her box seat to watch the show. She didn't care about the other acts on the card. All she cared about was Raine.

Finally, they were allowed to go in, and the show started. LaJuan occupied her mind during the first performances. The people near her were annoying. Some of the men tried hitting on her, and she shut them down one by one. She had matured. There was a time she probably would have taken one of them home and slept with him, but since Kyle and the birth of her daughter, she was a different person.

She valued herself. She realized that her stepfather was a pervert, and she did nothing wrong to deserve that treatment. After she left Kyle, she promised that no man would have her again unless she was married to him.

Finally, Raine's performance started. She was magnificent. LaJuan stood up and shouted throughout the show. The man next to her said, "Oh, so you're a lesbian? I get it now."

LaJuan rolled her eyes at him, "What are you talking about?"

The man continued, "Well, you didn't respond to any of us, but as soon as she came out, you're jumping up and down. You must like women."

LaJuan cheered for Raine. The music went low as she prepared for a slow song. LaJuan eased over to the man, "No, honey, I'm not a lesbian, but I am a coldhearted killer. Talk to me like that again, and I'll make you disappear."

The man was stunned. LaJuan winked her eye at him to ensure him she meant what she said. She laughed as he pushed his way out of the room and away from LaJuan. She mumbled, *"That'll teach him to mess with me!"*

A woman behind LaJuan tapped her on the shoulder, "Hey thank you for that. That jerk was getting on my last nerve, girl."

LaJuan high-fived the lady, "Mine too, but he's gone, thank goodness!"

The ladies laughed and continued to enjoy the show.

After the show, LaJuan stood around the room and small talked with some of the people. She didn't normally do this, but she had nothing else to do so she hung around. After a few minutes, her heart nearly stopped. Raine walked into the room and started shaking hands with people.

LaJuan's surveillance skills worked for her. She hid her face and made her way out to the door in an attempt to avoid Raine. She got to the door and heard Raine's voice behind, "Hey, wait! Come back!"

LaJuan beat it out the door and down the hall as fast as she could. She looked behind her, but no one was following her. She thought, *"That was close, but why did I run? I should have stayed there and talked to her. Maybe we could have patched things up. Oh well, time to go home and get ready for my mission."*

***

LaJuan was rolling down the street in her drop-top, letting the breeze blow through her hair. She was mentally preparing for her next mission. First things first, she had to go check in on her daughter then pay the

Pastor another visit. She still couldn't believe she told so much about herself in the last meeting. She wondered if she would get to the point of telling him about the men in suits. She wondered if he would even believe it.

She got to the street where Kim lived. She hoped to catch a glimpse of her lovely daughter. She missed her so much. She just wanted to hug her one more time, but she knew that could be dangerous for Kim. She didn't care about her own life, she just didn't want her daughter to suffer her fate.

She eased down the street, and there she was outside, playing with some of the other kids. Kyle's mom didn't know her, so she thought of playing lost just to get closer to Kim. She stopped the car and walked into the yard, smiling at the girls playing. They all waved at LaJuan and LaJuan said, "Hi, girls. Have fun."

Kyle's mom came up to her, "Can I help you?"

LaJuan smiled. Kyle looked so much like her, "Yes, I'm lost. I'm trying to find Westover Drive. Can you help?"

Kyle's mom answered, "Oh, sure. If you go down a block and turn right then go straight, you'll run right into it."

LaJuan smiled even harder pretending to appreciate the help, "Thank you so much! The girls are so pretty. All of them yours?"

Kyle's mom answered, "Oh no, sweetie, the one in the red and black is my granddaughter, and the others are her little friends."

LaJuan said, "Well, they're all beautiful."

Kyle's mom replied, "Thank you, dear."

LaJuan responded, "Thank you again and have a blessed day!"

"You too, sweetie!"

LaJuan smirked at the thought of telling someone to have a blessed day. She didn't believe in blessings at all, so why bless someone else's day? It was all a game she played. She knew if she used buzzwords like that, it would make people feel at ease around her. They would trust her, and she could then get what she wanted from them.

She remembered her training even included using Christian terminology to seduce people into trusting her. Once, she even prayed for a group of people, luring them into her web. When she gained their trust, the men in suits ordered her to poison them. She laughed at the thought of people trusting a trained assassin.

She pulled her car into the back alley of the church and went inside as she usually did. The secretary greeted her and sent her to the pastor's office. It always went down the same way. That was something LaJuan actually appreciated. Routine was good for someone who broke their routine on purpose so much.

As usual, Pastor Ponder was on the phone. He was a very busy man running one of the busiest churches in the city. She listened to his conversation and laughed inwardly at how he sounded more like a businessman than a pastor. She thought, *"I guess that's the nature of churches these days!"*

He finally hung up the phone, and they went through the usual pleasantries. Then Pastor Ponder asked, "Are you ready to share with me what you do for a living?"

LaJuan giggled and thought, *"I must be getting relaxed around this man. I'm giggling like a little girl."* She said, "I don't know if you can handle it."

Pastor Ponder placed his arms on the desk and folded his hands together. He was a stout man with graying hair and a chiseled face. He took a deep breath and patiently said, "As I've said before, your secrets are safe here. I will not divulge anything you tell me. My only goal here is getting you the help you need and saving your soul."

LaJuan was serious, "My soul can't be saved."

Pastor Ponder nodded his head, "Yes, it can. There is nothing you have done that can't be forgiven unless you've lied on the spirit. Have you?"

LaJuan thought it for a moment. Of all the wrong things she had done in her life, she couldn't think of a time that she did that, "No sir, not that I can think of anyway."

"You probably haven't. You can be saved right here, right now in the room. We can gather a few more people together, and you can be saved."

LaJuan could tell he was growing agitated with her, but he didn't know the things that she had seen and done in her life. If he knew, he wouldn't be talking to her now. She looked him in the eyes, "You don't know the people I work for and the things that I have done. If you did, you wouldn't be saying that."

Pastor Ponder held his head down and sighed, "Honey, it doesn't matter. You can be saved, and that's all that I need to know. If you repent, acknowledge Christ as your Lord and Savior, and give your life to him. You will be saved."

LaJuan laughed, "That's the funny thing, Pastor, it's not my life to give. I don't own it anymore."

Pastor asked, "What? No one loses the right to their life. It is yours and yours alone."

LaJuan wanted to tell him. She wanted to tell him about the people she worked for, but that would endanger his life. She knew it was a mistake to go there, and she decided to get out of there now before someone was needlessly killed. She liked Pastor Ponder because he was like a father to her. She missed her father so much, and this man reminded her of him. She couldn't endanger his life.

She quickly stood up, "I have to go. Thanks, Pastor."

Pastor Ponder stood up with her and held out his hands. She walked around the desk and hugged him. He said, "I'm here for you whenever you're ready."

LaJuan smiled. She believed she would never be ready. Her life belonged to Satan, and she had no control over it. She had to continue killing for them until they killed her. She walked out of the office and noticed that Channel was unusually perspiring. She paused for a second but decided to leave, not wanting to cause a commotion for Pastor Ponder. She had a mission to get ready for, but after that, she would come back and have a heart-to-heart with Channel.

3

Three days later...

The abandoned building sat across from a prestigious hotel in the downtown area. She didn't know how long she had camped out in the room, but she knew her target would be arriving soon. Her orders were clear—let there be no doubt that this was an assassination.

She checked her scope one more time to ensure she had it set properly. It was. She just waited, watching the people on the street going about their business. She thought, *"These idiots don't even know that I can take them all out right now if I wanted to. I control their fate, not the God they believe in, me...LaJuan Craig."*

She thought about Pastor Ponder and the things that he said to her during her counseling. He did make sense of the God and Jesus stuff, but he didn't know the reality of the world. He didn't know that Satan himself was running things on Earth, and she worked for him. She signed her name in blood, and that meant she no longer owned her soul.

She wondered what Kim was doing. She didn't want her daughter to end up in the same life that she was living. She hoped that keeping her far away from her would keep her safe from this existence. Not everyone was meant to see her dark side of life. Only a few could see it, and they were trapped in it forever. That is everyone except Raine Davis. She had escaped. She was one of the lucky ones.

The limo pulled up to the hotel. LaJuan recognized it as her target's limo. She readied herself to take the shot. She was a master at this. Her breathing was precise and controlled. She could even slow her heart rate.

Just three years before, she had taken a shot from 400 yards away from her target. She hit him center mass, killing him with one bullet. That was her proudest moment.

Two people got out of the limo, both of which LaJuan recognized as assistants for the target. She knew he would be next. She set herself, looked through her scope. The rifle sat on the smooth edge of the circle she cut in the glass. The target got out of the limo and shook hands with people.

LaJuan slowly squeezed the trigger. Instantly the shot hit the target in the head, splattering blood over everyone standing near him. People screamed. LaJuan loved to hear their screams. It meant she was successful—the target was dead.

She slowly packed up her gear and left the room. Outside, she saw all the commotion in front of the hotel. However, no one would suspect a sexy looking African-American woman wearing a tight skimpy skirt and a revealing blouse would be an assassin. But she was, and she was the best in the business.

She casually walked to her limited-edition, candy apple red Lamborghini, calmly got in, started it, and drove away from the scene.

The phone rang, and she immediately answered without looking at the caller ID, "It's done."

She knew who it was, and they got the message. She was successful again as always. She flipped off her wig and tossed it in the back seat. At the light, she picked her real hair into a nice afro. Going natural gave her a different look, and she enjoyed it. She smiled with pride and drove off into the sunset.

***

Alone again in her lavish uptown condo, LaJuan sat and watched the news on television. She smiled as the reporter told the story of how one of the world's richest businessmen was gunned down in broad daylight. The reporter added that there were no leads to who the shooter might be, and LaJuan snickered, "And there won't be either, hun."

She leaned her head back against the wall and sighed. When she raised her head back, the news was now reporting on entertainment's biggest singer, Raine Davis. Raine's fourth album was a platinum release, and they were showing highlights of her performing on stage at her pre-release concert.

After Raine lost her sister, Penny, she moved to a new record label and started her career over. She refused to sing any of the songs from her first album. LaJuan resented her back then and wanted to kill her, but the men in suits wouldn't allow it.

Initially, LaJuan would scout Raine, hoping for an opportunity to take her out, and the men in suits wouldn't know it was her who did it. However, she remembered what happened to her aunt and thought better of it. They would know, they always knew. Then she came to realize that she loved Raine, and she really couldn't have hurt her. Raine was a kindhearted person, and LaJuan hated the fact that she got everything. But she loved her friend now, and one day she would try to fix their relationship.

LaJuan had one secret in this life, and she couldn't tell anyone. Kim was a masterpiece, and she lived to keep her daughter safe. She knew if the men in suits found out her secret, they would use it against her.

She brought up her favorite video site on her smart TV. She had several videos on the site and often watched them. This particular video had sentimental value to her because it held her secret. No one would know it because LaJuan filmed it at a place where she was executing a contract. Anyone watching the video would think she was planning to assassinate someone.

She played the video several times smiling more and more each time. It was her greatest enjoyment, and she only wished she could go back. She wondered how life would be as a normal person, but she knew she was far from normal. *"Normal people don't sign contracts in blood. Normal people don't kill others. Honey, I miss you so much."*

The one thing she admired about Raine was that she got out of her contract. Maybe that's the same reason that at times she hated her so much. *"Raine got all the breaks in life. Even when we were kids, she got all the breaks. Everyone loved her, but no one cared one bit about me. I didn't get noticed until I killed my rapist. I hate her, but I love her too. How stupid is that?"*

She did love Raine. In becoming her friend, she found herself like so many others, falling for Raine's charismatic charm. She knew how to turn it on. *"Damien had a good woman, but he was too stupid to realize it."*

She drifted off to sleep as one of Raine's videos played in the background. She found herself calling out, "Raine...I do miss you, my friend."

***

The next day, LaJuan woke up still on the sofa. She hadn't moved all night and had a slight hangover. She cleaned herself up and decided to head out for some coffee to help ease the hangover.

She walked out of her building and stopped traffic. Men were staring at her as they always did. She was stunning. This particular morning, she was enjoying the attention. She didn't understand why, but it made her feel some type of way. Maybe she was feeling what it was like to be Raine. Halfway down the block, a woman brushed into her and knocked her purse off her arm. LaJuan stood over it, looking at her with piercing eyes.

The lady was profusely apologizing, and that annoyed LaJuan to no end. LaJuan said, "It's okay, it's quite alright." She bent down to pick up her purse and the items that fell out of it. A bullet hit the window beside her, breaking the glass. LaJuan was stunned. Someone was trying to kill her, and the lady who knocked her purse off her arm saved her life. Coincidences like that didn't often happen for her.

She surveyed the buildings across the street, hiding behind anything she could. Another shot landed near her. Now, she knew she was the target. She managed to get her purse and pull out her Glock. She narrowed the choices of where her shooter could be hiding, aimed, and fired several shots. People ran everywhere, hiding anywhere they could. She heard sirens in the distance. She knew the shooter would be leaving his position.

She used that moment to dart in the coffee shop's front door, toss her phone in the trash, and dart out the back door. She had to make her way to her safe house with her stash of identities. Whoever was trying to kill her wouldn't give up. She knew that because if it were her, she wouldn't give up.

She managed to get back to her building and to her car, but something wasn't right. She felt something was wrong. That eerie feeling made her look around her car. She got on her knees and looked under the car. She saw a red light blinking under the car. The wires ran up to the ignition, and she knew what would happen if she started her car. At some point during the night, someone rigged her car to explode and set up an assassination attempt on her. They knew her car, her condo, and her routine.

She slowly got up and looked around. Someone was trying to take her out, and her mind was racing to figure out who it was. Was this a response to the assassination of the businessman yesterday or was it someone from her past? She didn't know, but she had to get off the grid, regroup, and figure things out.

She couldn't go back to her condo because she reasoned they would either be there or have a trap set up. She pulled off her heels and continued to survey the garage. She found a late model sedan and smashed the window. She chose a late model car because it would be easier for her to hotwire.

She unlocked the door and jumped into the car. She pulled out two wires and scraped them together. Nothing happened the first two times, but the car fired up the third time. She closed the car door and pulled off toward the exit.

She got out on the street and noticed two men in suits standing across the street from the garage. She sped off as fast as she could without getting a ticket. The men in suits weren't following her, so she didn't know if they were sent to kill her or if someone else was after her.

She drove around several city blocks until she was sure no one was following her. When she was sure, she headed outside the city to her safe house. She set the house up five years ago and had not visited since then. The house contained clothes, money, and a completely new identity for LaJuan. She kept this for emergencies, and she was in the midst of one now.

She parked about a mile away from the safe house. She didn't want to take any chances. If her attempted assassins were as good as she was, they would have thoroughly researched her and possibly found this location. She walked through the wooded area and off the main path, paying close attention to everything around her.

She heard nothing and saw nothing. She could see the house in the distance, and no one was around it. She still remained cautious, not wanting to take any chances with her life. She got to the house and closely looked around for any devices and traps. There were none.

She went inside the house. It appeared no one had been there for a long time. She went straight to the floorboard in the living room and pulled up two planks. Underneath, she found her documents, two guns, money, and three burner phones.

She pulled out everything and put the items on the table. She went to the bedroom closet and picked out a new outfit. She put it on with a blonde wig to disguise herself.

She pondered the notion of who could want her dead and could carry it out. She had assassinated hundreds of people, but most, if not all of them, didn't even know their loved ones had been assassinated. Whoever was after her knew she was an assassin. They knew exactly where she lived, what car she drove, and even what type of coffee she loved.

She took a deep breath and thought, *"The only people who know me this well and could pull this off are my employers, the men in suits. Why would they want me dead? I've not crossed them in any way. At least not yet. They must have found out about my meetings and discussions at the church. I'm willing to bet Channel had something to do with telling them. She'll have to pay for that."*

She didn't want her call to be traced, so she decided to take her spare car and drive to another location. Once there she would call the office and find out some information. She looked around carefully, making sure she didn't leave anything. She would not be returning to this location again.

***

LaJuan pulled up to a vacant parking lot. She could see for miles around, so no one could take a shot at her or sneak up on her. She pulled out one of the burner phones and dialed the office number. The receptionist answered, "One World Government, may I direct your call?"

LaJuan coldly replied, "LC dash 1789."

The receptionist responded, "Thank you, just a second."

The phone went dead and then rang again as it usually did. After two rings, someone answered, "Are you safe?"

LaJuan knew they knew what was happening to her, "Yes, I'm safe. What's going on, and who's trying to kill me?"

"It seems our database isn't secure, either. Someone hacked our network and obtained the information on who filled the contract for yesterday. They must have sold this information, and that person is after you."

It was a reasonable answer, but LaJuan couldn't believe that the computer network of the most powerful organization in the world was hacked, and its information was stolen. Her gut told her that something wasn't right, but she decided to play along.

"What should I do?"

"Continue to lay low while we track this person down and terminate them."

"Yes sir."

The phone went dead, and LaJuan tossed the burner. She couldn't go back to the safe house, so she determined the best thing to do was to go somewhere no one would ever suspect.

4

Kyle Coleman was the best at hacking into computer systems. He was so good that he managed to hack his way around and find information about his former girlfriend, LaJuan Craig. What he had learned wasn't good, but it helped him understand why she ran from him and their daughter. He implemented everything LaJuan told him, too, to keep their daughter safe.

He drove up to his mother's home to see his daughter. Sometimes he would stay away for days before coming to see Kim. He also kept his routine as irregular as possible. He didn't want anyone following him and learning about Kim.

He arrived at his mom's house, and Kim came running to him, "Daddy!"

"Hey baby, how are you?"

"I'm fine, Daddy. I missed you."

"I missed you too, sweetheart." Kyle's mom came in after Kim. Kyle said, "Hey, Momma. How are you today?"

"I'm fine, baby. You sister called a little bit ago. She said she's coming back in later today."

Kyle smiled. He loved his sister Andra. They were half brother and sister, but they never referred to themselves as anything but brother and sister. He said, "Great, it'll be good to see her."

"Yeah, maybe we can all do dinner tomorrow."

"That's fine."

"Have you heard from your baby momma?"

Kyle frowned at the comment, "No, Momma, but I told you I wouldn't hear from her again."

"Son, what kind of woman runs out on her child..."

"Momma, please don't go there. There's a lot about her that you just don't understand."

Kyle's momma sighed, "You still love that heifer?"

Kyle rolled his eyes. Kyle's momma continued, "Who are you rolling your eyes at?"

Kyle chuckled, "Yes, Momma, I do still love her, and I'm praying that one day she will come back, and we can be a family. I know you don't understand, but I do understand, so just trust me."

"Son, I do trust your mind, but you're thinking with your heart on this one. It's time to move on. That Vanessa girl is nice. Why don't you take her out?"

"Okay, time to go. Take care, Momma. Give me a hug, baby."

Kim jumped up into her dad's arms and gave him a hug. Kyle's momma said, "Bye, son. You take care of yourself."

***

Kyle was driving back to his office. He ran an IT company with some of the city's top contracts. His team was highly skilled. His most trusted friend Al was calling him, "Hey Al, what's up?"

Al said, "We've been hit?"

"What? What are you talking about?"

Somebody came in here and shot up the place. Calvin and Jake are dead."

"What? Why would anyone want to shoot up my place?"

Al said, "I don't know, my brother."

Kyle ordered, "Get out of there and head to our..."

The shots rang out around Kyle's vehicle, breaking the driver's side window but missing Kyle by centimeters. He quickly spun the car around and jumped out the door. He ran as fast as he could down the sidewalk. There was yelling and screaming going on behind him, but he didn't stop to look. He kept running and thinking about the plan LaJuan had him set up just in case something like this happened. He was angry then, but now he was very appreciative of it.

5

LaJuan found a small, quaint coffee shop on the east side of town, a part of town she never frequented. She was well trained and knew better than to go to any of her routine places. She played the sequence of events over and over in her head trying to figure out who wanted her dead. She kept coming to the same conclusion—the men in suits.

Sure, the explanation provided by the leader made sense, but she knew their operation and couldn't believe someone could hack their network. They had the top-of-the-line of everything, and no one was even bold enough to try and hack their system.

She decided to contact some people she knew had the skills to hack sophisticated networks. Kyle was one person she trusted unequivocally. She planned to track him down and talk to him. She didn't want to call him and risk her call being intercepted.

She finished her coffee and took a bus and a train to Kyle's office. When she arrived, she saw police everywhere. Something happened, and bodies were carried out of the building. LaJuan was worried that Kyle might have been attacked and killed.

She got closer to see who was killed. She eased over to one of the people from the coroner's office and asked, "Do you know who was killed?"

The woman answered, "Yeah, two young IT guys. They say some men came in and shot up the place."

"Oh, when you say young, how old were they?"

The woman thought for a second then said, "Probably 22 or 23, something around there."

LaJuan was happy. It couldn't have been Kyle because he was 34. LaJuan said, "Thank you." She moved away and headed to one of Kyle's hangouts.

After a short drive, she went into the Internet bar where Kyle liked to hang out and looked around but didn't see him. Kyle often went there to work during the week and to hang out on weekends. Any traces of him would lead back to the café and not to his office.

She left the café and walked five blocks to a game room that Kyle often visited. She walked around the room, turning the heads of every male in the room. LaJuan smirked as she knew so many guys lusted for her body, but none of them cared about her mind. She was 35 years old now and was done playing games. She didn't have the time or the life that would include a relationship. She hadn't had sex in over a year but didn't miss it.

Kyle wasn't there, either. She was running out of options. There was one last place she could look, but she didn't want to go there. His headquarters was on the east side of town, but if she were being tracked, she would lead them there. She decided to wait and see if he showed up at the game room. If not, she would have no choice but to go to his headquarters.

She sat down at a table. It wasn't long before someone tried their luck. She thought he was attractive, but she didn't have time for it. The man sat down and smiled, "What's your name, beautiful?"

LaJuan smiled back and said coldly with little emotion, "I don't have time for this so have a nice day."

The man continued to smile and nodded his head, "Come on baby, you're sitting here all alone. What's the harm in telling me your name?"

She leaned forward slightly with less emotion than before and quietly said, "Maybe I didn't make myself clear. I said I don't have time for this, so please leave."

The man angrily got up, "Whatever, you ain't all that anyway."

LaJuan snickered and thought to herself, *"They all say that when they get rejected."*

She continued to wait when another man sat down and looked her squarely in the eyes, "I see you're sitting all alone, so I decided to come over and keep you company."

LaJuan said, "I'm alone because I choose to be, so please leave. I'm waiting for someone."

The man chuckled, but LaJuan could tell he wasn't really laughing, "I know you are, but he won't be coming."

LaJuan perked up, "What?"

He put his hands on the table and leaned forward. LaJuan eased her hand inside her purse. She was ready to take him out if necessary. He said, "You won't need that Glock. Anyway, I have you covered every way."

LaJuan looked around, and the man was right. She was trapped, but she calculated that she could take two of the men out quickly and her skill could get her out of the building. She wasn't worried.

She said, "Really. Make a move, and we'll see."

He chuckled again, "No need for that. You're probably waiting for Kyle Coleman, but he won't be coming."

LaJuan tightly gripped her Glock and put her hand on the trigger, "Who are you?"

Now his smile seemed real, "Kyle was right, you are good but so am I. I'm someone who wants to help you, so you can take your hand off your weapon."

LaJuan knew this one had skills. He must be in the business, "How do you want to help me?"

The man introduced himself, "I'm Albert Jackson, Kyle's cousin. He won't be coming because someone tried to kill him earlier, so he went into hiding. He suspected it was you, so I came here to see if you would show up here. My boys have their guns pointed at you. I'm helping you by telling you this and giving you a chance to leave and stop pursuing my cousin. If you persist in trying to kill him, well, I'll have to kill you." He smiled and continued to stare LaJuan in her eyes.

LaJuan replied, "I'm not the one trying to kill Kyle. Why would I kill him? Someone tried to kill me earlier, and I came here to get Kyle's help on a lead."

Albert's eyebrow rose, "He thought you might be trying to get Kim back. So, who do you think it is?"

LaJuan smiled, "Let me let you in on a secret, I wouldn't need to kill Kyle to get Kim back. She's better off with him anyway. Lastly, I love Kyle and would never raise a hand to him. But one thing is for sure, I would kill anyone who threatens him or my daughter. Understand?"

Albert raised his eyebrow, "Clearly."

LaJuan took her hand out of her purse. She believed she could trust Albert. Although she wouldn't readily admit it, he won her respect as someone who was in the same business as she was. "I have my suspicions, but I'd rather talk to Kyle. Him I trust, you I'm not sure."

Albert pulled out his cell and dialed the number, "Yeah, she's alone." He handed the phone to LaJuan, "Hello."

"Hello, baby, are you trying to kill me?"

LaJuan smiled. It felt good to hear his voice after all this time. She missed him so much, but she didn't dare come to see him or Kim. She said, "If you know me then you know that I wouldn't have failed. Now, is this line secure?"

Kyle snickered into the phone, "If you know me, you know it is. Go with Al. He'll bring you to me."

LaJuan hung up the phone and followed Albert out of the game room. She knew she could completely trust Albert because Kyle always ran deep background checks on anyone he worked with. Albert had to be checked to be his number one. Also, if Albert wanted her dead, he could have easily tried it already.

As LaJuan walked out of the game room, a man smiled at her strangely. She thought she recognized his face, but she wasn't sure about it. She knew he wasn't a threat, but something was calming about him.

***

LaJuan and Albert arrived at a building off of 2nd Street in Ybor City. They went into one of the back rooms. The entrance was secured with a retinal scanner. Once inside, LaJuan saw Kyle sitting at a computer. Finding Kyle sitting at a computer was all too familiar to LaJuan. Her heart skipped a beat when he smiled. That was something no other man could do for her.

The two hugged as if they hadn't seen each other in a while, which was true. She longed for him many nights but couldn't go see him. He took away all the deep-rooted pain she felt in her life. She didn't know how he did it, but he did. She loved him, and now she was glad to see him again. Unfortunately, it wasn't the best time. LaJuan asked, "Someone is trying to kill you as well?"

Kyle answered, "Hello to you too, baby. And yes, someone is trying to kill me. What's going on, LaJuan? I know I've hacked some things in my day, but no one has ever wanted me dead for it."

LaJuan deeply sighed. "Is there somewhere we can talk alone? I need to tell you a few things about me."

Kyle paused, "I already know about you and what you do. Remember I'm a hacker. I found out right after you left."

LaJuan said, "You still love me?"

"Never stopped."

The response touched LaJuan's heart. This man still loved her despite her career choice. She said, "So why would someone want you dead?"

Kyle shrugged his shoulders, "Beats me. I haven't even hacked anything of any worth lately, at least that I know of anyway."

LaJuan noticed a picture on Kyle's computer. She picked it up and smiled, "How is she?"

Kyle took the picture from LaJuan, "She's fine and safe from any of this."

LaJuan frowned, "What, you think I don't deserve to look at her pic?"

Kyle sighed, "No, I don't think you do. You left us, and that's not something I can easily forget. Anyway, why are people trying to kill me? Does it have something to do with you? I'm sure it probably does."

LaJuan nodded, "I don't know. Someone tried to kill me, also. You need to make sure Kim is okay."

Kyle turned, "She's fine. I did as you asked and made sure no one knows about her. Anyway, since when do you care about my daughter?"

LaJuan didn't want to tell him that she knew he had done as she asked because she checked on Kim every chance she got.

LaJuan said seriously, "Stop it, she's my daughter too. I dIdn't ask for this life. I left to keep you both safe."

Kyle said sarcastically, "That seems to be working out well."

LaJuan frowned, "This isn't the time to argue. If this is about me and they're trying to kill you, then that means they're trying to kill me and any family I might have. They obviously know about our history, and that's what made you a target. Make damn sure Kim is safe."

"I have." Kyle sat back down at his computer and began punching up video footage, "Where were you when they tried to kill you?"

"On my way to the coffee shop on Saint Stephens drive near the Montrose apartment building, but the shop doesn't have any cameras."

Kyle smiled, "You still don't get it, do you? There are cameras everywhere." He looked up at LaJuan, "Your career must pay well for you to live in that ritzy place."

She didn't respond. She didn't like the fact that he found out that she was an assassin, but there was nothing she could do about it. If the men in suits found out he knew, they would surely kill him. She thought, *"I guess it doesn't matter now."*

Kyle swung back around, "Hang on, and let's see what we can pull up." He pecked away at his computer and then pulled up some camera footage, "Here we go. Now, let's see."

LaJuan watched the video, "There I am right there." She studied the video, looking at the background. It got to the point where the shots were fired, "Stop it." Kyle stopped the video, "Now can you pan upward about 45 degrees to that building?"

Kyle followed her instructions and LaJuan saw something in the window of the building where she believed the shots were coming from, "There, now can you zoom in on that point right there?"

Kyle zoomed in. "Can you clean that up a bit?"

Kyle said, "A little." He cleaned the picture up the best he could.

LaJuan said, "Still can't make it out. Do you have any facial recognition software?"

Kyle and Al laughed. "Come on baby, do you know who we are?"

LaJuan coldly responded, "Run it."

Kyle rhetorically looked at her. She said, "Please."

Kyle started the process and leaned back in his chair, "This could take a minute." The computer clicked as soon as he said it.

"Whoa, maybe not...let's see."

LaJuan said without emotion, "That's not possible."

Kyle turned and looked at her, "What do you mean?"

"He's dead." She turned and walked toward the door.

Kyle shouted, "Hey, where are you going?"

LaJuan sternly replied, "I have business to handle. Make sure you stay safe and keep my daughter safe."

Kyle said angrily, "You're ducking out on me again. I will keep my daughter safe."

LaJuan stared at him, "Kyle, I'm doing this to save you and Kim. You don't understand these people. They will stop at nothing to kill anyone associated with me. They want me dead, and nothing on this Earth will stop them. They will come for you and possibly Kim—if they know about her—as their way of getting me to come out, so they can kill me. Just give me some time to figure this out and end it."

Kyle stood there. LaJuan could tell he was hurting, but she couldn't take the risk. She had to do it alone. She asked, "Can a sister get a car, a clean one?"

Kyle tossed his keys to her and LaJuan caught them. Kyle said, "It's clean, brand new papers and a clean VIN number."

"Great." She walked out of the building and towards the car. Each step showed a stern determination. She now knew who was trying to kill her and why. She just didn't know how he obtained the skills or the nerve to do it. She also knew he couldn't be after her without the permission of the men in suits. They were all behind it, and if necessary, she would kill them all to save Kyle and her precious daughter, Kim.

6

"Yasssss!" Raine was celebrating the release of the rankings for her new album, "Pleasing Raine." It debuted at number one. It had been five years since she lost her oldest sister, but her career hadn't suffered. Neither had her love life.

Raine and Jay were husband and wife now, and she enjoyed her new life. She missed her sister and couldn't go a day without thinking of Penny. She was happy that she and Nya were as tight as two sisters could ever be, though. She called Nya virtually every day.

Jay walked into the room, "Hey, baby, we still going to breakfast?"

Raine, "Yes, look at these rankings, sweetheart. I'm number one!"

Jay smiled, "Come on, girl, did you really think you wouldn't be at the top? That's where you belong."

Raine put her hand on her hip, "Are we talking about music, Jay?"

Jay laughed, "I'll meet you by the car."

She loved him so much. She couldn't understand how she could have allowed herself to marry Damien. Jay was everything she ever wanted in a man. He was kind, considerate, and loved her more than anyone could ever love a woman. She would never make a mistake like that again.

Raine's oldest daughter Penny came running into the room, "Hey, Mommy!"

Raine answered, "Hey, baby! Daddy is taking us to breakfast."

"Yayyyy!"

"Go put your shoes on and wait for me at the front door."

Penny ran to get her shoes while Raine grabbed her shoes and her youngest child, Jay Junior whom they called JJ.

Everything was going well for Raine, and she couldn't imagine living like she did with Damien. Today would start with breakfast, then she would meet with her team, and the rest of the day she could spend with her husband and kids. Life was great.

***

Raine was sitting by the pool and watching the news on the nearby television. Jay and Penny were playing in the pool. Raine stared at Penny. She thought she looked like her big sister. She was glad she named her after Penny. Even at four years old, Penny could sing with the best of them. Raine knew she had talent and would someday be like all the other Davis women.

The news started reporting on the shooting that occurred in the downtown area. Raine jumped up when she saw LaJuan in one of the shots. She rewound the TV and watched it several times to be sure it was LaJuan.

She hadn't seen her since she escaped her contract with the men in suits. She thoroughly believed LaJuan worked for the men in suits, but she never found out for certain.

She wondered if LaJuan was the target or just happened to be there at the time. The reporter didn't say who the target of the shooting was, but she suspected it was LaJuan. It was too much of a coincidence for her not to be the target.

She decided not to give it any more thought. She didn't want anything to ruin her day. She got up, removed her robe, and dived into the pool. She swam across the pool and back. When she got close to Jay and Penny, she splashed water on both of them. They splashed water back on her, and the whole family began to have fun.

Raine's phone started ringing. She got out of the pool and went to answer it. It was Nya, "Hey girl, how's Florida life?"

Nya calmly replied, "Life is great, girl. How are you guys doing?"

Raine said, "We good. How's my daddy?"

"Daddy's doing great, baby girl. You almost can't tell he had the strokes."

Raine happily replied, "That's great! I can't wait to see y'all again."

Nya asked, "Did you see the report about the shooting out there?"

Raine completely changed, "Yeah, I saw it. I think that was LaJuan."

Nya replied, "I thought that was her. What do you think she's into?"

"The same mess she's always been into. She had me truly deceived, but you want to know the crazy part? I still like her and consider her a friend."

"Wow, Raine, why you feel that way?"

Raine sighed, "Well, I think deep inside she doesn't want to be that person. At times, she showed me that she really cared. For a minute, she got Damien off of me, but then she turned around and slept with him. I just think she's confused."

Nya said, "Well, you remember what happened to her in the projects, right?"

Raine perked up, "You know, I didn't even know that was her. Remember I was only about six back then."

Nya replied, "Yeah, I was only ten myself, but Daddy reminded me of the story. It was a shame what her stepdad was doing to her. I couldn't imagine being in her shoes. It's no wonder she turned out the way she did."

"Well, she never even mentioned it to me, so I guess she didn't consider me that close of a friend."

"She's probably not comfortable, Raine, so don't be so quick to judge."

"You're right. Well, I hear your nephew crying, so I better go show him some love."

"Okay, girl, tell both of them I love them, and Auntie will see them soon."

"Okay, Nya, take care girl."

"You too!"

Raine hung up the phone smiling. It was great talking to her sister. They were miles apart physically, but they were closer than ever mentally.

***

Raine dropped her kids off with the sitter. Jay was at work, and she wanted some time for herself. She stood at the sitter's door and prepared herself to run to her car. The rain was beating down on everything outside.

Her sitter said, "Kind of ironic, isn't it...Raine trying to beat the rain." She laughed, and Raine chuckled. Raine had heard that or something similar all her life, so it really wasn't funny anymore.

She said, "Yeah, see you later!" Raine put a sweater over her head and darted off to her Lexus. She wished she could mentally tell the car to open her door but laughed at the thought. She quickly got in and drove off.

Raine arrived at her favorite coffee spot and ordered her caramel macchiato and sat down at her favorite table. The store blocked this area off for stars, and Raine had a standard spot reserved.

She enjoyed the limelight, but sometimes her fans worked her nerves. She loved them and understood their excitement over seeing her, but at times she just wanted to be left alone with her favorite drink to enjoy life. This was one of those times.

Halfway into her macchiato, she was startled, "Hello, Raine. How are you?"

Raine couldn't believe her eyes. She didn't know what to say.

The man continued, "What—nothing to say?"

She finally said, "I...I thought I saw a report saying you were dead. Excuse me if I'm a little shocked." She was worried also. She didn't know what this man wanted, but she was glad she was in a public place.

"Well, the reports of my demise were greatly exaggerated."

Raine was confused, "But you were shot in the head, how could you be alive?"

The man smiled, "You don't need to know any of that. All you need to know is that I am alive, but LaJuan won't be. I'm going to kill her."

Raine was visibly nervous. Was he planning on killing her, too? She thought she had left that life behind, and now it was back at her door again.

He continued, "Don't worry, Raine. I have no beef with you. That is unless you're hiding LaJuan. I just wanted you to know that I wasn't dead. I also wanted to tell you that I was secretly in love with you. I didn't like the way Damien treated you. Since he's dead, well, maybe you and I can hook up after I take care of LaJuan."

Raine was disgusted. There was no way she would ever be with a man like him. She quietly said, "I'm married with two kids. I married the man I should have married before Damien. I'm sorry, but we can never be together."

He smiled, "Accidents happen."

Raine was truly shocked, "Please don't do this to me. I'm out of that business."

A man came up and stood at the table. He said to the man talking to Raine, "You were warned."

The man stood up, "See you around, Raine."

Raine jumped up, "Don, please leave my family and me..."

The man in the suit stood between Don and Raine. He held his hand up, "He won't bother you again."

The man turned and walked away. Raine couldn't believe Don had come back into her life. She had to warn Jay. She thought this was all over for her, but somehow it was coming back. Now, she was worried about her husband and kids.

7

LaJuan knew the person trying to kill her, but she couldn't imagine Don would have the nerve. He must be backed by some powerful people. Probably the same people she worked for, but why would they allow him to kill her?

She had to catch him and interrogate him to find out. Was he working alone, or was he working for the same people? She went to her headquarters building and took up a position where she could see anyone who entered the building. Not many people went into that building because it was owned by the most powerful people in the world.

She prepared herself to wait for hours. She was trained for this type of surveillance. She once waited in the same spot for ten hours for a target to appear, so this was nothing new for her. She pulled out her phone, put in her earbuds, and listened to Raine's new album.

It was only a 20-minute wait before Don and two men entered the building. Raine was right, he was working for the same people, and they must have wanted her dead. She leaned against the wall and tried to think.

"How can he be alive? I know I put a bullet in his forehead. Anyway, I know he wants revenge, but he's not going to get it."

LaJuan got up, gathered her things, and went downstairs. She couldn't go back to her employers because they were trying to kill her, and she didn't dare go back to Kyle out of fear of them learning his secret location. They did try to kill him as well, so they must know she has a connection with him.

She only hoped they didn't fully know what that connection was because she feared for him and Kim more than she did for herself. That was something she wasn't used to feeling. In all her life, she had never cared for someone else more than she did for herself. She decided to go somewhere that no one would think to look for her.

***

LaJuan took several buses and cabs to make sure she wasn't followed. She had to be very careful because the people she was dealing with had eyes everywhere. If they got her cornered, they would surely kill her.

When she arrived at her location, she went in the back door. Whenever she went there, she would enter through the back because she was afraid of anyone seeing her going into the building.

Once inside, she quickly realized where she saw the man from the game room before. He worked in this building. She remembered seeing him a few times but never had a conversation with him.

She quickly went into the office to speak with her counselor. As soon as she walked into the outer office, the receptionist looked at her surprisingly, "Miss Craig...uh...um...how are you?"

LaJuan quickly suspected she was the one who told the men in suits her secret. She thought about reaching into her purse, pulling out her gun, and killing her on the spot, but out of respect for God, she didn't. Pastor Ponder startled LaJuan, "Sister Davis, how are you today? We don't have an appointment, do we?"

LaJuan never took her eyes off the receptionist, "No sir, we don't. I need to speak with Channel for a minute."

Pastor Ponder looked at Channel then LaJuan, "Okay, I'll be in my office."

LaJuan leaned down and put the palms of her hands on the desktop, "You told them, didn't you?" Channel was clearly nervous and didn't respond. LaJuan turned her head slightly, "I know you did. It's written all over your face. You have put my life and the life of my friends in danger. The only reason I don't kill you now is out of respect for this church and Pastor Ponder."

"I won't tell them anymore, I promise. Please don't hurt me." She started to cry profusely, "They knew you were coming here and wanted to know what you were talking about to Pastor Ponder. They paid me good money, and I needed it. I was about to lose my house and everything. I have three children, please don't kill me."

LaJuan didn't want to kill her, but she feared for the lives of everyone she knew. She couldn't even stay in the church because of this woman. She had to go somewhere else now.

LaJuan said, "Give me your phone."

Channel reached into her purse and handed LaJuan her phone. LaJuan asked, "Is this how you were instructed to contact them?"

Channel meekly answered, "Yes. Whenever you were here, I was instructed to dial a number, give them a code, and tell the person that answered everything you told Pastor Ponder."

"How would they know what I told the pastor?"

"I left the intercom open whenever you were in there, so I could hear everything."

LaJuan believed her because she had several informants of her own, and they all followed the same procedures. If nothing else, the men in suits weren't very creative. They used the same formula for everything.

She went behind Channel's desk and ripped the phone cord out of the wall. She looked sternly in Channel's eyes, "I'm going in here to talk to Pastor Ponder. If you make any move to contact anyone, I will kill you and your family. If you know anything about me, then you know I will do it. Do we understand?"

"Yes. I won't move, I promise."

LaJuan knew Channel was terrified. LaJuan had no intention of harming her or her family. She just wanted to make sure Channel was sufficiently scared not to do anything while she talked with her pastor.

LaJuan strutted into Pastor Ponder's office, never taking her eyes off of Channel. Channel never looked back at her, either. She looked down and sniffled the entire time.

Pastor Ponder stood up and offered LaJuan a seat. LaJuan gently sat down. Pastor Ponder asked, "Are you okay? I saw you on the news. They're trying to kill you, aren't they?"

LaJuan answered, "Yes. Apparently, your receptionist was bribed into telling them about me and why I was here. Don't fire her, the people I work for can be very intimidating."

Pastor Ponder nodded his head, "I am so sorry, Sister Craig. What can I do to help?"

"There's nothing anyone can do. Twenty-one years ago, I got myself into this mess. Now I am the only one who can get myself out of it...or die trying."

"Well, we can't let that hap..." Channel came running into the office, "LaJuan they're here! I don't know how, but I just saw them on the monitor. I swear I didn't do anything."

LaJuan jumped up and looked at the monitor in Pastor Ponder's office. She saw Don and some other men get out of an SUV. Don looked slightly different than he did five years ago, but it was him."

She turned to Pastor Ponder, "Take me to that secret exit you told me about."

Channel said, "I promise I didn't tell them! Please don't hurt my family."

LaJuan smiled, "I was never going to hurt you or your family. I just needed to talk to the Pastor again and wanted you scared enough not to do anything. Go to your family and get them out of the city. They will come after you."

Channel ran out of the room, and Pastor Ponder led LaJuan to the secret passage. She thanked him for all of his advice over the last six months. She knew they were trying to kill her because she wanted to get her life in order. She knew it would come to this, and she was relieved that it was finally happening. She would either be free of the men in suits, or she would be dead.

***

LaJuan ran down the back alleys until she couldn't run anymore. She slipped inside a building and eased down the hallway. She heard voices. It sounded like people were revving up for something. It was some kind of meeting. People were clapping, welcoming the speaker. Someone tapped LaJuan on the shoulder, and her instincts told her to turn and strike.

She saw an elderly lady standing behind her and was able to hold off from punching her. Instead, LaJuan pretended to smile, "Hi, I'm lost or something."

The elderly lady said, "Nonsense come on in, baby. We're all friends here."

LaJuan and the lady walked into the room, and the elderly lady announced, "I found someone hiding in the hallway. She's a little afraid to join us, so let's give her a big Markus Foundation welcome!"

Everyone stood and clapped for LaJuan. People were tapping her on the shoulder and hugging her. LaJuan hadn't been shown so much love before in her life. The things Pastor Ponder said to her over the past six months appeared to be coming true. She took the first step to God, and He appeared to be coming all the way to her.

The elderly lady guided LaJuan to a seat, and she sat down. Another lady tapped LaJuan on the shoulder and asked, "What's your name, hun?"

LaJuan rolled her eyes at her. She didn't want to give her name to anyone. The lady continued, "We need it for your sticker sweetie."

LaJuan smiled, "Oh sorry, my name is Amy."

The lady wrote the fake name on the sticker and taped it to LaJuan's chest. LaJuan looked around, and everyone had names on their chest. She wondered if they were all fake names like hers.

The speaker started to make her speech, welcoming LaJuan in the process. LaJuan was so good at pretending to be someone that no one could tell her name wasn't Amy.

LaJuan thought she would be bored in a room filled with women talking about domestic violence. She wasn't a victim of domestic violence and didn't care, but when the speaker turned to child abuse, she started to listen.

The speaker talked about her experience with child abuse and how the foundation was founded because of an incident early in her life. At that moment, LaJuan's eyes started to fill with tears. She thought of her experience as a teenager—how she was abused by her stepdad and how her mom allowed it. She remembered how her mom got angry after she killed her stepdad. It angered her so much that she killed her mom as well.

Then the men in suits came to her rescue, but they really didn't rescue her. They turned her into a killer for hire—a killer for them. Every man she knew used her. Every man but one, Kyle Coleman. He was the only man who didn't use her. Instead, Kyle loved her and cared for her.

She had to get to him and protect him. He didn't know what he was up against, but she did. The speaker was finishing her speech and asked if anyone had any questions. It wasn't long before LaJuan realized that everyone in the room had a story. Most of their stories were similar or worse than hers.

The problem was that she killed her abusers, and none of the women in the room could manage that statement.

The speaker asked LaJuan, "How about you, Amy, do you have anything you'd like to share with the group?"

LaJuan was very uneasy. She was not going to talk about her past, so she quietly answered, "No ma'am."

The speaker smiled a reassuring smile at LaJuan. LaJuan felt relaxed. This was a place where she could lay low for a while, but she was worried about Kyle. She had to find a way to talk to him without being discovered.

The meeting ended, and everyone went to have refreshments. LaJuan asked the speaker, "Can I talk to you alone for a minute?"

She answered, "Sure." The speaker turned to the lady in charge and asked, "Is there a place where we can talk?"

The lady guided them down a hallway. The route took them past rooms that were used as sleeping quarters for the women. She realized that she had stumbled into a women's shelter. As long as she didn't use her real name, no one would know she was there. She smiled inside.

They arrived at a private room that appeared to be the lady's office. Once inside, the lady excused herself, and the speaker motioned to LaJuan, "Please have a seat." They both sat down, and she continued, "Now, what can I do for you?"

LaJuan eased back in her chair, "I know you. I mean, I know of you. You probably don't remember me, but I'm sure you remember my story."

The speaker looked puzzled, "I don't think I know you. This is my first trip to California in years."

"We didn't meet in California. Is everything I say confidential?"

The speaker answered, "Absolutely. We do not allow any information to leave this facility and personally what someone says to me in private stays private. The worst thing that could happen is to have your abuser track you down because we released information. That's a lesson I learned firsthand years ago."

LaJuan said, "I know you from Belmont Heights. Twenty-one years ago, I killed my abusers. My stepdad was constantly raping me, and my mother allowed it. I reached the point where I wanted to do something about it. Damien Black encouraged me to kill him. I thought about it before, but I never really believed I could do it until he encouraged me."

The speaker was intently listening to the story, but something in her eyes let LaJuan know she remembered the story. LaJuan continued, "So the last time he tried to rape me, I stabbed him in the side. My mother was angry because I killed her cash cow. I went and got the gun from her room and shot her."

LaJuan smiled, "I remember you because you were Markus Black's girlfriend. We never met personally, but I remember how you made him feel. He loved you, and he was one of the few good guys in this world."

LaJuan could tell she was happy to hear that. This woman reminded LaJuan of Raine. They had similar features, and their personalities were close. She didn't appear to be a person who craved fame, but she was passionate about fighting abuse.

"Do you remember my name?"

"Renata Smith. I remember you started the Markus Black Foundation along with Markus' sister Kyanna. Ky was such a sweet kid. I hoped she would never know the pain I went through. At least, I felt that way for a time, then I didn't care who suffered. I suffered so why shouldn't everyone suffer."

Renata said, "Well, I hope your presence here means that you've had a change of heart."

LaJuan sighed, "Actually, I'm here by accident."

Renata smiled, "There are no accidents in God's world."

LaJuan smiled back, "Okay, if you say so."

Renata smiled, "I do."

"Yeah, you can say that. If I told you the things I've done in my life, we could be here a very long time. Needless to say, I've not been a good girl."

Renata replied, "Well, you have time to change. If I remember correctly you're only a couple of years younger than me. You can change and even help others change."

LaJuan said, "I have started to change. I've spent the last six months getting counseling from a pastor. Because of that, my life is in danger. The people I work for are trying to kill me, and I'm out of places to lay low."

"I'm sure you can stay here. We can make that happen."

"I'm not a victim of anything."

Renata sat up in her chair, "Honey, you are a survivor of child abuse. It doesn't matter how long ago it was, you still had to endure it. We can make room for you here and get you help. I know a couple of very trustworthy police detectives we can contact."

LaJuan chuckled, "No police. You don't know the people I work for at all. The police don't stand a chance against them. I just need to lie low for a couple of days until I get a plan together. I don't need the police or anyone else, so please don't involve them. If you do, I promise you people will die."

"You can't solve your problems by killing people."

LaJuan smiled again, "I'm all done killing. People will die at the hands of my employers as they try and kill me. They don't care who gets in their way."

Renata said, "Okay, we'll work it your way. I am scheduled to leave town in the morning, but I will stay a couple of days to make sure you are situated. For now, let's go out and enjoy some refreshments with the group."

LaJuan nodded. All she needed was time to lay low, and now she hoped by telling some of her story to Renata that she would get time. She asked again, "No one will know my story or my real name, right?"

Renata smiled, "Honey, I will die with that secret. I lost the one man I loved because of abuse, so I know first-hand what it's like to lose someone. I won't ever tell your story or your name."

LaJuan asked, "Do you know it...my real name?"

Renata answered, "At first I couldn't remember, but isn't it LaJuan?"

"Yes." Renata put her arm around LaJuan, and they walked to the dining area. LaJuan felt at ease. For a couple of days, she should be safe.

8

Don confronted Pastor Ponder and Channel in the church. He was angry that LaJuan wasn't there. He wanted his revenge, and he was tired of wasting time chasing her around town. If that lady walking down the street hadn't bumped her, she would have been dead.

Don said, "Pastor, I'm getting tired of asking you. Where did she go?"

Pastor Ponder replied, "You can ask all day and night, but my answer would be the same, I don't know where she went. She left here without telling me. You know her, I'm sure you know she wouldn't make a mistake like that."

He was right. LaJuan wouldn't be careless and let the pastor know where she was going. However, she was slipping. She had become soft, and Don knew it. The LaJuan of five years ago would never seek the advice of a pastor. She didn't know the first thing about church, and now she was secretly talking to him, even threatening to leave the organization.

Don nodded, "You're right, she wouldn't." He looked at Channel, "You didn't tell us she was here. In fact, you warned her that we were here, didn't you?"

Channel plead, "No...I didn't say anything to her...please!"

Pastor Ponder shouted, "Leave her alone!"

Don pushed the pastor back and grabbed Channel, "If you don't want anything to happen to you or your family, I suggest you stay out of this matter."

Pastor Ponder just looked at Don. Don pulled Channel out of the church and pushed her into the car. The car sped off down the road.

* * *

The car pulled over to the side of the road, and one of the men in suits got out. He opened the back door where Don and Channel were sitting. Don handed him Channel's limp body. The man dragged it over to the embankment and tossed it over the side like a rag doll. He got back in the car, and they drove off.

Don and his henchmen arrived at his apartment building. He was still angry that he didn't get his revenge. He sat down on the couch and reviewed documents that he had assembled in his search for LaJuan. He had her routine schedule down, but he knew she wouldn't stick to it. She was somewhere that no one would expect her to be. He believed she was on foot, so she couldn't be far.

They had all the airports, buses, and trains covered, but she could easily drive out of town. He reasoned that she wouldn't do that because she wanted to know who was after her. The cover story the men in suits provided to him would hold up, and she will resurface at their headquarters. He would have to wait for that moment to get his revenge.

He continued reviewing the documents of LaJuan's history. Something kept nagging at him about all of her history. He felt it was staring him in the face, but he couldn't put his finger on it.

His cell rang, "Hello."

"Still no sign of her. Wherever she is, she's staying off the grid."

Don deeply sighed, "Keep tracking down that boyfriend. She'll turn up sooner or later."

"He's good at covering his tracks."

Don sternly replies, "Be better!"

"Yes sir."

He hung up the phone and continued to think. He thought back on his life and remembered growing up in Progress Village, a community in Tampa, Florida. He remembered how he met Damien in the boys' group home, and they immediately became friends for life. He just didn't think Damien's life would end so soon.

He did try and warn Damien not to try to kill Raine, but he wouldn't listen. Damien thought he knew it all, but in the end, he didn't. He thought, *"When this is all over, I'm going to kill Raine's husband and get that for myself. Damien didn't know how good he had it, but I sure will. I'm going to knock that out every night!"*

He slowly started to drift off to sleep, imagining different ways to kill LaJuan. He hated her more than he used to love her. At one point, she was the world to him, but she had no feelings for him at all. She used him, and when she was done, she tried to kill him. He thought about raping her then killing her, but he didn't even want that. He just wanted her dead and by the quickest means possible.

It delighted him that the men in suits were even paying him to kill her. He asked for the opportunity years ago, but they wouldn't allow it. Now that they speculated she was trying to leave the organization, they gave him permission to kill her, but it had to happen before she gave her life to Christ. Don laughed at the thought,

"LaJuan saved...they must be joking. That girl doesn't know the first thing about God or Jesus!"

9

LaJuan was sitting in the office with Renata when Kyanna came into the room. They stared at each other. LaJuan remembered her, but Kyanna was only ten when LaJuan went to reform school. LaJuan didn't think she remembered her.

Kyanna hugged LaJuan. She said, "Girl, it's good to see you again."

LaJuan smiled, "You remember me?"

"I don't by looks but more so by incidents. I do remember Markus crying because he knew you were suffering. He was like that. He cared more about others than himself. I also remember your fling with Damien, and from what I understand, it happened again later."

LaJuan said, "It's not something I'm proud of...either time."

Kyanna replied, "I'm not judging you. My brother was a jerk, and he killed the one man who loved me. I could never have forgiven him for that."

LaJuan nodded, "How's your former sister-in-law?"

Kyanna smiled, "Funny, she's the only good thing that came out of that marriage. Raine is great. Every time I'm in town, she invites me over. She treats me like a real sister."

LaJuan nodded again, "That sounds like Raine. Good to the core."

Renata said, "Well Ky, we have to get her settled in here. She's using the name Amy, so we need to get used to calling her that while she's here."

Kyanna replied, "That works for me." She turned to LaJuan, "If there's anything I can do, please let me know."

LaJuan responded, "There's one thing...could you ask Raine if she'll see me?"

Kyanna had a blank look on her face, "Well, I can ask. I'm meeting her in an hour for dinner. I will ask her then."

LaJuan replied, "Thank you. I truly appreciate that."

Renata and Kyanna walked LaJuan to her quarters and left her there to get comfortable. LaJuan was able to adjust to any sleeping situation. At times, she had the best living arrangements, but at other times, she lived in some hell holes. It was the nature of an assassin's job.

She sat in her quaint room, planning her next move. The shelter would work for a couple days but not forever. She had to do something. She couldn't live the rest of her life this way. She had to strike back, but first, she had to make sure Kyle and Kim were safe.

***

Early the next morning, LaJuan woke up and headed to the nearest coffee shop. Coffee was her vice. She had to have her cup first thing in the morning and from one particular chain of coffee shops. She wondered if it would be her undoing.

She sat down to enjoy her cup and thought about Raine. Raine refused Kyanna's request to meet with LaJuan and rightly so, given what LaJuan did to her. Raine was a good person, and LaJuan hated the way she treated her. She had never had a friend that was truly a friend to her until she met Raine.

If she did nothing else in this world, she would have to make things right with Raine. She would beg if she had to, and that wouldn't be easy for LaJuan.

Renata and Kyanna both came into the coffee shop and sat down with LaJuan. LaJuan knew they were angry with her for sneaking out of the shelter.

Renata smiled and nodded her head, "You just can't help yourself, can you?"

LaJuan dropped her head, "Well, some things I just can't help. I needed my coffee."

Renata said, "Being a creature of habit can get you killed."

LaJuan threw her head back, "No one knows this game better than me. I know who's after me now, and that gives me an advantage. I'm not one to sit still and hide. I'm the type to go after my problems and resolve them if you know what I mean."

Kyanna replied, "You can't keep living this life, LaJuan. God doesn't want you to live this way."

LaJuan laughed, "God...just like I asked Pastor Ponder, where was God when I was being raped virtually every night, huh? Where was he then? He didn't love me then, and he doesn't love me now."

Renata emphatically said, "That's not true, LaJuan. God does love you. I can't explain why you went through what you went through, but he was there then, and he's here now. You think that bullet missed you by accident? No, my friend, it missed you because God ordained it to miss you."

LaJuan just stared at Renata. She couldn't understand why this woman who barely knew her just called her "friend," and secondly, she made more sense than the pastor did. That bullet should have killed her, but the woman bumped her at the right time, saving her life. She asked herself, *"Could it have been God?"* Then she thought, *"No, just a coincidence."*

Kyanna added, "LaJuan, we don't have all the answers for why and what God does, but we trust him with all our hearts. My brother and mother died right in front of me, but I don't question why. Instead, I know they are in a better place. My mother was beaten more days than she had peace. Now she doesn't have to worry at all."

"But your brother...you have to ask yourself why?"

"I did ask myself why but look at what we've accomplished in his name. We have a nationwide organization that helps battered and beaten women become survivors. We have shelters all over the county designed to take women and children in and get their lives back in order. We're helping thousands of people each year, all with my brother's name on the organization."

"But he's dead, and you can't tell him you love him anymore."

"I tell him I love him every day. Just because he's not on Earth doesn't mean I can't tell him I love him."

LaJuan laughed, "You guys can't be real. I know the harsh life, and what it's all about." She leaned up to the table, "I've killed so many people I can't even count them. I've been raped, beaten, and slapped around so much that I think I'm immune to it. In the end, people are nothing to me. I've only had one real friend in my life, and I dogged her. I can never be saved."

Renata said, "Acts 22:4 says, 'I persecuted this way to the death, binding and delivering into prisons both men and women...' Paul was like you, he killed and imprisoned believers until God brought him into the body. If God can call Paul to stop killing his people, then he could do the same for you."

That touched LaJuan, but her feelings and emotions wouldn't let her show it. She didn't want to believe that she could be saved. Even after all the conversations she had with Pastor Ponder, she didn't want to believe it. Instead, she continued to fight against that nagging feeling that kept tugging at her. It was a feeling that someone was calling her to do something.

LaJuan stood up, "Thank you, ladies, for all your kind words. I have to track down my friend and make sure he's safe. If I don't see either of you again, well, it was nice talking to you."

Renata stood up, "LaJuan, wait...Let us help you."

LaJuan smiled at each of them, "Where I'm going, you can't help me. I'm either going to kill them, or they're going to kill me. That's just my life. Bye."

She walked away. This time, she wasn't garnering all the attention of the men in the shop. She speculated that it was because Renata and Kyanna were there as well. The three of them were all stunningly beautiful ladies set on different paths in life.

10

Raine often sat in her home relishing the quiet morning. This was one of them. She dropped the kids off with Jay's mom, and Jay was at work. She had to go down to the record company in a few hours, but she could peacefully relax without any noise for a minute. Raine loved her family, but there were times she wanted to be alone. This was one of those moments.

She thought about Kyanna's plea for her to speak with LaJuan. She wondered if LaJuan was truly a changed person or if it was some type of play to get next to her again. She laughed inwardly because if she hadn't run into Don, she would have agreed to the meeting. But seeing Don again brought up too many memories, and she didn't want to go back down that road.

The plea still bothered her, though. What could LaJuan want? Was she trying to pull her back into that secret world?

There was no way Raine was going to allow that to happen. Penny had given her life for Raine to escape. She was not about to go back.

The phone rang and broke Raine's thoughts. She answered, "Hello."

"Hi, Raine, this is Renata. I know you don't really know me, but I was just calling on behalf of LaJuan. She could really use a friend right now, so I was wondering if you would change your mind and at least talk to her."

Raine didn't want to say anything. After a pause, Renata continued, "Raine, are you there?"

Raine spoke calmly, "I'm here, and I do know who you are. I admire your work with the foundation. Maybe one day I can even come to one of the shelters and speak to the ladies."

"That would be awesome, Raine!"

"But as for LaJuan, I really can't see her right now. She's a reminder of a bad time in my life, and I really don't want to go back there. I've had one peek back at that life recently, and I don't need another one."

"I do understand but Raine, LaJuan is at a place where I think she can be saved. She acts like she doesn't believe it, but I believe she can be saved. She's trying to be tough, but something sent her to church to talk a pastor. That's what got her in her current situation. That organization she works for is afraid she'll quit and turn to God."

Raine was surprised to hear that about LaJuan. She was far away from God, and now, she's been seeking spiritual advice from a pastor? That didn't sound anything like LaJuan.

"LaJuan has been talking to a pastor?"

Renata answered, "Yes, and she is really on the verge of being saved."

Raine pondered the thought, "My fear is for my family more than for myself. Like I said, I've already had a visitor from my past threaten my husband, and LaJuan popping up isn't a good thing. I hope you understand my position."

"I do understand, Raine, and your family's safety is paramount. You're a saved woman, anointed by God, so please just consider what you could do to help save this woman's life."

Raine considered what Renata was saying. Saving LaJuan would be a great thing, especially knowing first hand where LaJuan came from. The sting of betrayal from someone who was once considered her best friend still hurt, but inside, Raine was the caring soul that couldn't help herself. She had to help. She thought, *"What would Penny do?"*

Renata asked, "Will you think about it, Raine?"

Raine answered, "Yes, I'll give it some thought."

"That's wonderful, Raine! I'm in town until tomorrow, so I would be honored to help facilitate a meeting. You can reach me at 555-377-3617. Thanks so much, Raine."

Raine could feel her smile and happiness through the phone, "Not a problem but remember, I said I'd think about it."

Renata replied, "I remember, and that's better than a flat out 'no.' Be blessed, Raine."

"You too, Renata." Raine hung up the phone and smiled. She enjoyed talking to Renata. She admired her motivation for building up the foundation in honor of her boyfriend.

Raine chuckled at the irony of all of them meeting back up. When she married Damien, she didn't realize that Damien was the one who killed his brother Markus. After she lost Penny, all of the past started coming out.

She remembered the story from her childhood, but she was only six at the time. She didn't know any of them because they were much older than she was, but when it started coming out, it sent a chill up her spine. Now the only member of the Black family left was Damien's sister

Kyanna, someone Raine admired and loved as a sister.

Raine sat down in her favorite chair. The music was pleasing to her ears, and she felt relaxed. Her eyes began to close until she was startled by a visitor, "Hi Raine."

"This can't be," thought Raine. She stood to her feet and asked, "How did you get here?"

"I'm not really here, Raine, but I need you to help LaJuan. She is at a point where she can be saved, and your support will greatly help her."

Raine was stern, "Okay, this is a joke, and it isn't funny. You're not Penny! Come out and stop this now!"

Penny smiled at Raine, "Raine, it is me."

Her words were so comforting that they made tears come to Raine's eyes. She missed her sister so much and still blamed herself for everything. Could it really be her? Can she have one more chance to talk to Penny?

Penny said, "Raine, I have to go now. Please help LaJuan."

Raine shouted, "No, don't go! Please, Penny. I'm sorry for what I did. Please don't go."

Penny waved and smiled at Raine as she faded out. A noise startled Raine and woke her from her sleep.

She realized that someone was ringing her doorbell. She gathered herself and went to the door. When she answered, she was stunned, "What are you doing here? How did you get past the security?"

"Come on, do you really think your security could stop me? You're forgetting who I am, aren't you?"

Raine pursed her lips, "I could never forget you."

"Are you gonna let me in?"

Raine answered, "Come on in, LaJuan."

She stepped aside and let LaJuan into her home. She stared at her as if she didn't know what to say. It had been years since she talked to LaJuan, and the rush of all the memories of the worst six months of her life came back.

Raine asked, "What do you want?"

"Ohhh, so cold. That's not the Raine I remember."

Raine nodded her head, "Really, LaJuan, you worked for those men, you slept with my husband, and everyone believes you killed Damien and Don. But of course, Don isn't dead, so that one isn't right."

"How do you know he's not dead? Did you see him?"

Raine sternly answered, "Yeah, and he threatened Jay. It seems he has a crush on me. Why is it I keep attracting these idiots?"

LaJuan smiled, "You attract all men, Raine. You're a beautiful and talented woman so you can expect to attract the good guys and the bad ones."

This was not going like Raine expected. She expected a reunion with LaJuan to be loud and combative, but this reunion was quiet, and LaJuan was even complimenting Raine. Could she want something?

Raine sarcastically replied, "What do you want LaJuan? You've never been this nice to me. Not even when we were friends."

"I just want your forgiveness, Raine. I did some bad things to you, and I wish I could have done things differently. I knew what Damien was doing to you, and I stopped it for a minute, but I should have stopped it permanently. My pastor said that I was a psychopath."

Raine frowned, "Pastor? You? Right. I believe that one."

"I shouldn't say *my* pastor. I should say *a* pastor. I was talking to this pastor about my life and what I wanted to do. But anyway, he's right. I fit the definition."

Raine asked, "What's the definition?"

LaJuan toyed around with the statues on the wall, "Psychopathy is characterized as a complete lack of conscience regarding others. I would say that fits me totally, wouldn't you?"

Raine sarcastically replied, "Well, yeah."

LaJuan giggled, "You don't have to hold back, girl. I know what my problems are, and I certainly know where they came from, but I want to be free of it. I want to live a normal life like you and everyone else. That's why I was talking to that pastor. He thinks I can change, but he doesn't know the people I work for like how you and I know them. The only way out is death."

"There's got to be another way, LaJuan."

"Raine, the only reason you're standing here today is because Damien killed your sister. If he hadn't, you would be working for them or dead. It's that simple."

Raine sternly said, "God can get you out."

LaJuan sarcastically laughed, "God? Wow, all of you sing the same song but in a different key. God doesn't love me like he loves you, Raine. My only way out is death."

Raine seriously replied, "That just isn't true LaJuan. You're here because God wants you in his number."

LaJuan said, "Okay whatever. I'm going to get myself out of this, not God."

Raine walked over to LaJuan, "Then what do you want me to do?"

LaJuan smiled again, "If something happens to me, and if Kyle Coleman is already dead, then I want you to go to this address and get my Last Will and Testament. It's in a safety deposit box, and the combination is on the paper. In it, there are instructions for what you are to do next. That's all you have to do, follow the instructions."

Raine asked, "Is it legal? I'm not breaking any laws for you, LaJuan."

"It's straight up legal, girl. I wouldn't have you do anything against the law."

LaJuan patted Raine on the shoulder, "Thanks, Raine. I truly appreciate it."

Raine said, "Why did you ask Kyanna if you could come to see me if you were going to just barge in here anyway?"

LaJuan snickered, "Just trying to be polite, the new me."

They both giggled. Raine said, "I'm going to pray for you, LaJuan."

"Yeah well, I don't think there's a God that loves me, Raine, but thanks anyway."

Raine smiled and watched LaJuan walk out the door. Renata was right. She had changed. She wasn't the LaJuan that Raine knew five years before. Raine called Renata and let her know that she met LaJuan then she headed to her meeting at the record company.

11

Renata was sipping on some herbal tea when she heard the knock on her hotel door. She sprung up, excited to answer it. She got to the door and asked, "Who is it?"

"It's me girl, you know that."

She flung the door opened and hugged her best friend in the world, Andra.

"Hey, girl, how you been?"

Andra was all smiles, "I've been good, just trying to earn a little cash."

Renata put her hand on her hip, "A little? I know good and well a model of your statute makes more than a little."

"Okay, maybe a bit more."

They both laughed and hugged one more time. Renata said, "I thought I wouldn't get to see you, then something came up and allowed me to stay in town a little longer. I'm so glad we got this chance to connect again."

"Girl, me too, I got your message last night and couldn't

wait to come see you. After my show ended, I hopped on the first thing smoking and got here."

Renata motioned for Andra to sit, and she sat as well, "I have to tell you something."

"Me too, I have something to tell you."

Renata smiled, "I've been asked to run for mayor."

Andra stood up quickly, "What? That's awesome!"

"Can you believe it, me an elected official? Wow, I'm still wondering if I should do it."

Andra replied, "Girl, do it! You got my full support."

"Somehow...I knew that. What's your news?"

Andra sat back down, crossed her legs, and smiled, "I'm getting married."

"What? Omar finally asked the question?"

Andra smiled, "Yes! It was time. Our careers have gotten in the way long enough. It's time to make it happen, and of course, you're the maid of honor."

"Yasssss! Somehow I knew that, too! I'm so happy for you guys. That's great news."

Andra asked, "So what kept you in town so long?"

Renata pondered the question. If there was anyone in the world that she could and would trust, it was Andra. They had been friends since childhood, and there was never any hint of mistrust.

She deeply sighed, "You must keep this to yourself."

"Yeah girl, you know I don't roll like that."

"Okay, remember when we were kids, and that girl killed her parents?"

Andra's face turned serious, "Yeah, that was horrible what was happening to her."

"Well, I ran into her. She came into one of my shelters looking for help."

Andra was shocked, "Oh my God. Is she okay?"

"Well she's okay, but she is a piece of work. Her life is in shambles, but I think she is trying to give her life to Christ. She won't admit it, but I think she wants it. I also think something is motivating her to leave that life behind."

"You're helping her, right?"

Renata sighed, "Yeah, I am doing all I can."

"Well, that's all you can do. If anyone can help her, you can. Markus would be so proud of you."

Renata smiled, "Thank you, girl."

Andra asked, "So, how are things going with James?"

Renata replied uncomfortably, "Well, okay I guess. After all these years, it's still hard for me to allow myself to get close to someone. Every time I do, I keep seeing that dreadful day in my mind."

"You know Markus would want you to go on with your life, right? He was just that kind of guy."

Renata eased into a smile, "Yeah, he was. My mom tells me all the time that it's okay to go on, and James is a good man. If I went on, it would be with someone like him. I'm just going to continue to take it slow for now. I just hope he's patient with me."

"I'll be praying for you. You deserve a husband and a family."

Renata burst into laughter, "A husband? That's down the road girl."

Andra laughed with her, "I know, but I'm claiming it."

Andra's phone rang, "Hello."

The voice answered, "Hey, Andra."

"Kyle, hey, I was trying to call you last night. Where are you?"

"Look, Andra, I need you to do something for me. I sent you a secure message on that line I set up a while back. All the information you need is there, so just follow the instructions and don't tell anyone what's going on."

Andra gasped, "Kyle what are you into?"

"Someone is trying to kill me because of a girl I dated a while back. They know about my daughter, too."

Andra gasped again, "What? Kyle, oh my God, how could you put yourself and Kim at risk like that?"

"Look, this has nothing to do with me. I just had the bad luck of falling in love with the wrong person. Now, they are trying to kill her. They want Kim and me because they know we are the only people she truly cares about."

"Oh my God, I can't believe this is happening."

Renata put her hand on Andra's shoulder. Andra looked at her and tried to smile.

Kyle continued, "Andra, I have to get out of here and go deep into hiding. Get the message and follow the instructions. Most of all, get out of town. If they know about Kim and me, they might know about you."

He hung up the phone, and Andra stood there in shock. Andra looked at Renata with tears in her eyes, "Someone is trying to kill my brother and niece. Why would anyone want to kill that poor little child?"

Renata asked, "Why are they trying to kill him? Did he hack into something he shouldn't have?"

"Ironically, he didn't do anything wrong this time. They are trying to kill him because he's in love with the mother of his child. They want her dead, and he thinks they are after him because of what she feels for him."

Renata slowly sat down and listened closely to Andra. Andra continued, "This girl must have done something wrong to someone because now they want her dead along with Kyle and Kim. I have to get this message he sent me and see what he wants me to do."

Renata asked, "When did they try and kill him?" Andra was busy getting the message. Renata asked again, "When did they try and kill him, Andra?"

"Oh, I don't know, he didn't say."

Renata asked, "Who's the girl?"

"Don't know that either. He never told me the mother's name."

Renata said, "Andra, I think either two people have similar stories of someone trying to kill them and their loved ones, or LaJuan is the mother of your niece."

Andra quickly looked up, "What?"

"Yeah, she told a very similar story but just from her perspective."

Andra eased down in a chair in shock, "Wow, this just keeps getting weird. I have to go and get Kim, then go to a safe house and pick up papers for her. He wants me to take her to Nya Davis' house to live. I didn't even know he knew Nya."

Renata replied, "I didn't either. He must have kept it a secret for something just like this."

Andra responded, "I gotta go."

Renata said, "I'm going with you."

Andra stopped suddenly, "No, there's no reason for both of us to be in danger."

Renata sternly replied, "You are the best friend I have in the world. I'm not going to let you do this alone. I'm going too, and that's the end of it."

They both smiled at each other with reassurance. Renata knew Andra understood where she was coming from. If the roles were reversed, she knew Andra would do the same for her.

12

Kyle hung up his phone and pondered his situation. He loved LaJuan more than he would ever let her know. He knew she wasn't one to allow her feelings to come out, and it made him do the same. He admitted to his closest friend, Al, how much he loved her.

He sat and thought about his daughter. Kim was the most important thing in his life, and he knew if his big sister could get her away from his mom and take her to Florida that she would be okay.

The one person he didn't worry about was LaJuan. She could certainly take care of herself. When Kyle learned her secret, he couldn't believe it. He once saw a video of her fighting three men and taking them out with speed and accuracy. It amazed Kyle. She was as good with her hands and weapons as Kyle was with a computer.

There hadn't been any sign of the men who tried to kill him earlier, but that didn't mean they couldn't track him. Kyle knew it only took one misstep, and all their lives would be in danger. He wiped the computers of all the whereabouts of his daughter and anything related to the plan to get her out of town.

He removed the information related to his mother. However, the one thing he couldn't remove is the knowledge the people who worked for him held. He knew Al would die before he told anything, but he couldn't be so sure about the others.

Protecting Kim's whereabouts in the past only related to keeping her away from her killer mother, but now this was worse. LaJuan would never threaten Kim's life, but these men would. They would threaten and kill her and his mom. He hoped Andra would get to the house and save both of them.

He had to get to a place his team wouldn't suspect. He had a secure location set up in the city that no one knew about. He got up, grabbed his keys, and prepared to leave. He motioned to Al, "Hey man, I need to get out of here. If those men come back, they will want me, not you guys. I can't tell any of you where I'm going. Cool?"

Al responded, "Yeah man, cool. I got yo' back."

"If it's one thing I know, it's that. I wiped the computers, but that doesn't mean they won't torture anyone they

get their hands on. You'll have to make sure that doesn't happen. They can't find my mom and daughter."

Al nodded, "I understand. Get out of here, dude."

Kyle slapped hands with Al. Somehow, he knew it might be the last time he saw his best friend. He looked into Al's eyes and believed he suspected it, too.

Kyle got into a car and sat there for a minute. He was deep in thought; sad over leaving the people he loved. He almost didn't hear the sound of the bullets going off in the building he just left.

Kyle tipped back to the building and peeked in one of the windows. He could see Al on his knees with a big dude holding his chin and another man holding Al's arm. Much of Kyle's team was dead.

He couldn't hear what was being said, but the leader held a gun to Chase's head while he talked to Al. Al was clenching his teeth, slowly shaking his head. The pop of the gun scared Kyle. He had never seen anyone murdered live and in person before. Unfortunately, the first time had just been one of his friends.

The leader snatched Tina and roughly put her on her knees in the same position as Chase. Kyle suspected the same question was being asked, but this time, Tina

screamed something to the leader that seemed to please him. Al tried mightily to free himself, but he couldn't.

Tina led the leader to a computer and began punching some keys. Kyle wasn't worried because he wiped the computers clean of any data. A few seconds later, Kyle began to get worried.

Tina pulled up information that she must have saved in a partitioned drive of her own. Al continued to fight, but he was no match for the men holding him. The leader turned, smiled, and barked an order.

One of the men whipped out a gun and fired a shot to Al's head, killing him instantly. Kyle fell backward. He had to get to his mom's house before the men. He didn't know exactly what information Tina had, but he couldn't risk it. He ran to his car, hearing another shot in the background. Giving the information apparently didn't save Tina.

**

Kyle pulled up at his mom's house. There were no usual cars around, so he believed he had gotten there first. After all, he didn't know what the men in suits saw. He simply rushed over to get his mother and daughter.

He ran into the house, but no one was there. He looked everywhere. He didn't know what to do. He had to find them before those men found them. This was a time that he needed LaJuan. She would know what to do.

He ran out of the house and back to his car. He decided to drive a couple of blocks over and call his mom from her friend's house. If anyone saw the call coming in, they would only think she was getting a call from a friend.

Kyle pulled up in front of Miss Johnson's house. He had known her all of his life, so he trusted her. Kyle ran to the front door and knocked aggressively.

Miss Johnson came to the door, "Hey Kyle, how are you?"

"I'm okay, Miss Johnson. Have you seen my mom?"

Miss Johnson was worried, "Yeah, she left with your sister about an hour ago. They left out of here like a bat out of Hell. What's going on, Kyle?"

"Miss Johnson, I wish I could tell you, but if anyone comes around looking for them, please don't tell them what you told me. Please, Miss Johnson?"

"Okay Kyle, I'll just stay here to myself. You be safe, son."

Kyle was relieved, "I will be, Miss Johnson." He turned and ran back to his car. At least Andra was following the plan, but if Tina somehow knew the plan, then they would be in danger anyway. He still had to find them or find out what information Tina had given them. He rationalized that he would have to go back to the building to see what was on that computer. It should be safe now.

***

Kyle drove near the building. Police were everywhere. Now, he really had a problem. The computer was probably in their possession. He had an idea.

Kyle was a true computer geek. He knew all the codes to his system by heart. He got close enough to the building, so he could use his smartphone to connect to the Wi-Fi. Once he connected to the Wi-Fi, it was easy to connect to the computer. Fortunately, the last thing Tina looked at was still on the computer. She had Kyle's mother's address along with Andra and Kim's names.

He searched through her drive but found nothing that said she found out Kyle's plan for Andra. A police technician noticed someone was accessing the drive. Kyle quickly shut down the connection and got out of there.

Kyle sat in his car and watched the police work the scene. He knew all of his friends were dead because of his relationship with LaJuan. He loved her so much, but now, that love cost him the lives of so many. He cursed her name but prayed she was safe.

He set out for the safe house location, hoping to run into Andra and his mom. He told her to go there, use one of the disposable phones to contact Nya Davis, and get Kim to her. No matter what, Kim had to be safe.

While he was driving, he prayed that everyone would come out of this safely. He wanted LaJuan out of that business, and this situation made him want it even more. He knew she wanted it also, but she always believed she couldn't get out without dying. Somehow, he had to do something to get her out.

Kyle pulled up a half mile from the safe house. He learned from his hacking experience not to park directly in front of the safe house. Many of his friends had been arrested because they parked and walked right up to the house where the police were waiting. He made it a habit of parking away from any location, so he could scout things out first.

He tipped up to the house and decided to go around back to look in one of the windows. He looked in and saw his mother, Andra, Kim, and Renata. He was angry that Andra involved Renata in their situation.

He used his key and went in the back door and called out, "Andra?"

Everyone ran into the kitchen. Kim ran to her dad and jumped into his arms. She always completed him. She loved him no matter what, more than anyone else. None of his faults mattered to Kim. All she knew is that she loved her daddy.

Andra asked, "Are you okay, Kyle?"

"I'm fine. Why did you involve her?"

Renata quickly replied, "And hello to you, too, my friend."

"Hello, Renata. I didn't mean anything by it. I just didn't want you to get hurt."

"I totally understand what you're saying, but Andra is my friend. I will be there for her no matter what."

Andra added, "You see, I couldn't have stopped her if I tried."

Kyle's mom hugged him tightly, "Hey, baby."

"Hey, Momma. How are you?"

"I'm fine, baby."

Kyle looked at everyone, "Okay, we need a new plan."

Renata asked, "Have you heard from LaJuan?"

Kyle was surprised, "You know about us?"

Renata looked at Andra, "Yeah."

Kyle shook his head, "My sweet sister."

Andra said, "Hey, she figured it out. LaJuan came to her at her shelter."

Kyle asked, "She did?"

Renata added, "Yeah, she came to see me. She didn't know we were there. She just happened to stumble in there, running from those men. She left this morning on her way to see you."

Kyle said, "I haven't seen her, and now I'm worried about her."

Andra sarcastically replied, "Really? You're worried about a trained assassin?"

Kyle sighed. Andra continued, "She already knows that, too. LaJuan told her, so don't get all huffy with me, dude."

"Well, I'm still worried about her. There are more of them with guns than her, and well...I love her."

Andra's brow rose, "Really? I never heard you admit that before."

"Well, it's true. I want her out of that life, and frankly, I want to marry her."

Andra was surprised, "Oh my God. I thought I would never hear you say you'd marry anyone." Andra put her hand on Kyle's shoulder, "We'll find her, okay?"

Kyle nodded, but something inside of him didn't believe his big sister. He wanted to believe her, but this was a deadly situation, and all it takes is one bullet to end a life.

Kyle said, "We need to get Momma and Kim out of the city. They need to be safe before we do anything. In fact, all of you need to get out of the city. I'll track LaJuan down and figure this thing out."

Andra turned and looked at her mom, "Momma, take Kim and get out of the city. Kyle and I got work to do."

Kyle's mom said seriously, "I am not about to let my only two children go after trained killers to save another killer. We're calling the police."

Kyle quickly responded, "Momma, no! If we do that, we'll all be in danger. You don't know these people. The best play is for all of you to get out of the city. Take Kim to Nya. She'll be safe in Florida."

Andra said, "I'm not going. I'm staying here with my only brother."

Renata replied, "I'm staying with my best friend. Kyle, you need help. It's gonna be hard to get out of the city. I suggest your mom and Kim go to Raine's house. She will be safe there until we can get her out of the city."

Kyle responded, "That's a good idea. Do you think Raine will be okay with it?"

Renata smiled, "If I know Raine, she will be okay with it. As much as she tries to pretend she hates LaJuan, I believe she loves her and stills count her as a good, if not a best friend."

Kyle said, "Okay Renata, you take Momma and Kim to Raine's place, and Andra and I will search for LaJuan." Kyle retrieved the burner phones and handed two to Renata, "Here, take these phones. If you need to reach me, call me. I've already programmed the numbers into the phones. Use each phone only once. We can't risk it after that."

Andra asked, "How do you know so much about this?"

Kyle answered, "My girlfriend taught me just in case I was in a situation like this."

Andra replied, "Well, I guess that was a good thing."

Kyle responded, "Okay, let's do this. Renata, don't go directly to Raine's. Drive around until you're sure you're not being followed. Any questions?" No one had any questions.

Renata said, "Can we pray first?"

Everyone joined hands in a circle, and Kyle led them in a prayer for their safety.

13

Don stood in the center of the living room looking around, trying to get an understanding of the situation. He studied the pictures on the wall and ascertained that she loved her son and granddaughter. He reasoned that he must have just missed whoever came to pick them up. He was hot on their trail, and LaJuan couldn't be far from them. The taste of revenge kept him going. Nothing was going to stop him from killing her.

The scene made him think of his twin brother Daniel. Daniel was the nicest guy Don knew, and he wanted him to stay out of the business that he had gotten into. No one knew about Daniel because Don wanted him to stay safe.

LaJuan thought Don was visiting another woman, but it was really Daniel who was visiting her. He loved his twin brother more than anyone in the world. He remembered how they use to run game on different girls in the neighborhood. No one could tell them apart. When Don wanted to meet up with another girl, Daniel would cover for him with his main girl. During school, one of them would stay back in the locker room with a girl while the other took his place in P.E. class. They worked it any way they could until Daniel got in serious trouble.

One day, Daniel hooked up with a girl in the neighborhood, but she wouldn't have sex with him. Tried as he might, she refused, but Daniel wouldn't take no for an answer. He raped the girl, and she reported it to the police.

Don was the stronger twin and wouldn't let his brother take the fall. Instead, he took his place, and Don was sent to a reformatory school. In the school, he met Damien Black, and they became friends for life.

Don's lieutenant came up behind him, "She's not here. The kid or the old woman, neither of them are here."

Without turning to look at the man, Don replied, "I already suspected that. She's either with LaJuan or that Kyle dude. Let's get out of here and regroup before someone sees us."

Don walked to his car with two of his men. He slammed his fist on the hood of the car in anger. His lieutenant asked, "What do you want us to do now?"

Don stared out the window, "Nothing. She'll come to us now. If there's anything I know about this woman, it's that she will come after the person who's trying to kill her. All we have to do is be ready for her when she comes."

The lieutenant said, "You think she's that crazy?"

"LaJuan is not to be underestimated. She is a very skilled killer, and now that she knows we're after her, she will bring the fight to us. You can count on it."

Don leaned back in his chair and pondered. He couldn't wait to kill LaJuan. He reminisced about the nights that he spent with her. He was captivated by her love, but he soon realized that she was only using him. Until Kyle, LaJuan didn't care about any man, and that brought more rage to Don.

He dreamed of putting a bullet into her boyfriend right before putting one in her. He believed it would feel good. Nothing would satisfy him like killing her.

He thought about the night Raine's sister was killed by Damien. LaJuan always suspected Don had a girlfriend, and that was the first place she went to look for him. When LaJuan called upset with him, he knew she was going to kill him. However, she thought he was at the girl's house.

That's when he called his twin brother to warn him that LaJuan was outside. It was the worst call he could have made. His twin brother, Daniel ran out of the apartment and right into LaJuan. She killed him with one bullet to the forehead.

LaJuan had no idea that Don had a twin, so she thought he was dead. He couldn't act without permission from the men in suits, so Don decided to wait for his opportunity to get his revenge.

When he got the call, he learned everything about her and set up the kill. If it had not been for the lady bumping into LaJuan, he would have gotten his revenge already.

Now, he had to track her down. He planned to take his time killing her, savoring every moment.

The car pulled up to the headquarters building, and Don got out. He went inside to meet with the leader. He hated these meetings. The leader struck fear in him. He knew if he didn't catch LaJuan soon, the leader would have him killed. That's just the way things worked in the organization.

***

Don stood in the conference room as the leader, and his entourage walked in and took their respective places. They did everything the same as always. Don thought, *"If nothing else, they stick to the routine."*

The Leader spoke, "Did you track LaJuan down?"

Don fearfully replied, "No, we just missed her where the child was staying. We tortured the people at the hideout, but they only gave us the mother's address, and no one was there."

The Leader was angered, "You couldn't convince them to talk? Maybe we chose the wrong person for this assignment."

"No, you didn't. LaJuan is very good at what she does...probably the best. She's smart and skilled. She wouldn't have told them or anyone else where she was because she knew we would get it out of them. I do believe we don't have to look for LaJuan any longer. She knows we are looking for her, and that alone will bring her to us. It's just a matter of time."

The Leader stood and adjusted his jacket, "She'd better, or it will be a matter of time for you."

"Yes sir."

They walked out of the room as sharply and impressively as they walked in the room. Don sat in the chair for a moment. His lieutenant came in, "Are you ready?"

Don stood up, "In a minute."

LaJuan wasn't going to be easy, and that's why he wanted to take her out in a surprise blitz attack. That didn't work, so now he needed a plan. He needed to be ready for her when she arrived.

He stood up and walked past his lieutenant without saying a word. The man followed Don without question.

Don and his lieutenant got into their vehicle, and the driver asked, "Where to, sir?"

Don answered, "Oasis."

Oasis was the club Don often frequented. When he needed to think, he would go there and relax. He knew LaJuan remembered this location, and she might jump him there.

He wondered what Raine was doing. For years, he wanted Raine, but he didn't go near her because the men in suits had forbidden it. After he dealt with LaJuan, he was going to go after Raine. He would have to remove her husband and claim her for himself. He thought,

"Damien was stupid for losing that piece. If I had it, I'd know what to do with it and how to keep it."

He sat up quickly and snapped at his lieutenant, "Wait, Raine...I bet she's going to Raine's house and leaving the child there! Go get that child, and then we'll know for sure LaJuan will come after us."

The lieutenant jumped up, "Yes sir!"

14

After her meeting with Raine, LaJuan went back to Kyle's hideout. She was very careful to make sure she wasn't being followed. She took the long route, often going in circles to see if anyone was following her. No one was following her. She walked to the back door and saw the police tape everywhere. Something drastic happened, and LaJuan feared Kyle was dead.

She saw outlines of bodies and knew several people had been killed. For the first time in her life, she found herself praying. She prayed that Kyle wasn't one of the dead. He didn't deserve any of this. This was her life. She chose the life, Kyle didn't.

All the computers were gone. LaJuan didn't know if the police took them or if the killers took them. One thing was for sure—she had to act fast. She grabbed the keys to one of the vehicles and rushed outside. She clicked the remote until the beep led her to the car. She jumped in and headed down the road. If anyone were following her, changing cars would hinder them.

She was in full panic mode. She knew she had changed. She had never felt this way in her life, especially about another person.

She continued to think about Kyle. For so many years, she was emotionless, but this man made her feel something. She had sex with many men in her life, but this man was different. He made her know what love was about, and now, she feared he paid dearly for it.

Something rolled down LaJuan's cheek. She hadn't allowed herself to cry in years. Until now, she didn't believe she could cry. Men didn't mean anything to her until Kyle. She had to save the only other thing that mattered to her. She had to get to their daughter before Don got there.

She never thought much about Kim until today because she never believed she could be in her life. Now, all she wanted was to be a part of her life. She had to avenge Kyle's death and retrieve their daughter. She would find a way out of the organization to live a decent life with her daughter. She would even consider the God she didn't know. Maybe there was something to him. She couldn't understand why that woman bumped her at the exact time. That seemingly insignificant action saved her life. Maybe God did love her, but why let Kyle die? He didn't deserve to die.

She pulled up to a house in a small, quaint neighborhood. She selected this neighborhood because nothing about it was special. It was old-fashioned and charming. No one would think to look here unless they found the information on a computer network system of the best hacker LaJuan knew. Don had accomplished just that, and now she was scared.

She parked in front of a house down the street from the one she wanted. She got out of the vehicle and checked her weapon. She scanned the neighborhood and didn't see any suspicious vehicles.

She eased down to the house, trying her best to fit into the neighborhood scheme. It was hard because she dressed in a stunning outfit that brought out her best features. This neighborhood was for the married, archaic-dressed woman.

She got to the house she wanted and found the door opened. She looked around the neighborhood but didn't see anything out of order. She slipped in the door and looked around. Nothing was out of place, and no one was home.

She looked at some of the pictures on the fireplace and smiled. Kim was a beautiful little girl. She couldn't imagine how someone as bad as she was could have created such a beautiful person.

In one swift moment, she pulled out her gun, whipped it around, and aimed at her target. The elderly woman grabbed her heart and nearly passed out. LaJuan ran to her and grabbed her, "I'm so sorry. I didn't know it was you."

The older woman's tension eased a bit, "Oh my God, I thought you were going to kill me."

"No ma'am. I'm just here looking for my child."

The woman stared confused, "Your child? You're Kim's mother?"

LaJuan smiled. No one had ever called her that before, but yes, she was Kim's mother and proud of it, "Yes, do you know where they went?"

"Well, Kyle told me..."

"Kyle? You saw Kyle?"

The woman was shocked, "Yes, I saw him a few minutes ago, and he was afraid for his mom and daughter. After he left, some men came. They stayed for a while, I suspect looking for Kyle or Kim. Kyle told me not to let them know anything, so I didn't. Those men left a few minutes before you got here."

LaJuan was relieved that Kyle was still alive and that Kim was safe. She had to find her daughter and protect her from Don. If she knew anything about Kyle she knew he had a plan, and he was working on it.

"Miss, please don't tell anyone what you have told me and don't come back here no matter who comes here. Can I count on you?"

The woman was proud, "You sure can baby, and you be careful. Those men looked very dangerous."

LaJuan smirked. The woman didn't know how dangerous she was, but she would be careful because they outnumbered her. She simply said, "I will." LaJuan turned and walked out of the house and to her car.

The only man in the world she truly loved was still alive, but where was he? Where was her only child? She had to find them, and she had to do it quickly.

***

LaJuan went back to the shelter where she believed Renata and Kyanna were having their last session with the residents before they were to leave.

LaJuan eased into the building, and the receptionist recognized her and let her inside. She spotted Kyanna in front of the group speaking. She admired Kyanna because she was so fluent in speaking. The words just seem to roll over her tongue like they were made to do so. Speaking in front of large audiences wasn't something LaJuan relished. She preferred to speak one-on-one often with her prey.

LaJuan's mind wondered to Kim. That little girl had changed her life. From the moment she was born, LaJuan felt a change happening to her from the inside out. Again, she asked herself, *"How could something so perfect come from something so...so me?"*

Six months ago, she realized she had to get out of the business. Her daughter would never be safe as long as she worked for this organization. She had to get out or die. She never suspected they would go after Kyle first. Now the both of them were on the run somewhere, and she didn't know where they were.

LaJuan waited until the speech was over, and Kyanna came to her. Kyanna had a look of surprise on her face, "Hey, what are you doing here? Where's Renata and Andra?"

LaJuan asked, "Andra? She's in town?"

"Yeah, they went to find you and Andra's brother...Kyle or something."

LaJuan said, "Yeah, his name is Kyle. Where did they go?"

Kyanna answered, "I don't know. Renata was real secretive. What's going on here?"

LaJuan put her hand on Kyanna's shoulder, "It's best I don't tell you." She turned and left Kyanna standing there mystified. She knew if Don and his men came to the shelter and tortured her, Kyanna would tell him what she knew. It was best to keep her out of the loop.

15

Renata, Andra's mom, and Kim arrive at Raine's house. Renata avoided most of the small talk on the ride over, and Kim assisted by taking the mom's attention most of the time. Inside Renata was worried. She had never been in any situation like this before. When she was a teenager and Markus was going through his situation with his dad, she wasn't directly involved. She never really had to fear for her life. This time it was different.

These men were bent on killing LaJuan, and it seemed like they were ready to kill anyone associated with her. She wasn't going to allow her friends to go through this without her support, so even though she was scared and feared for her life, she was still going to help.

She jumped out of the car and didn't wait for Kim or the mother. She rang the doorbell and prayed Raine was home. Renata paced in front of the door waiting, still praying for Raine to answer, but she didn't.

Renata walked back to the car where the mother had gotten out with Kim. Renata said, "I guess she's not home. I don't want to go anywhere..."

"Hey...I was upstairs and thought I heard the doorbell. Y'all come on in!"

It was Raine, and Renata was relieved to see her. She thought she had to find somewhere to hide until Raine came home, but now they could stay here with her.

Renata went into the house and marveled at all the exquisite furnishings in Raine's beautiful home. Renata commented, "Wow, Raine, this is one beautiful home. I love that picture of your sister."

Raine replied, "Yeah, I put it over the fireplace because it's a special place to remind me of the sacrifice my sister made to save me. That night plays over in my head almost every night. I won't ever forget it."

Renata put her arm around Raine, "And you shouldn't. The love your family has for one another is boundless. You would have done the same for Penny. I'm sure she's up in Heaven smiling at the accomplishments of her baby sister."

Raine turned and smiled emphatically, "As I'm sure Markus is doing the same for you and your accomplishments. I'm so proud of what you have done in his name."

Renata turned her head to the side, "Well, your donations helped a lot too, girl!"

Raine said, "I can do more, and I will. What brings you guys here, and who is this little angel?" Raine moves over to Kim, "Hi, Miss Coleman, how are you? Where's Andra?"

Renata answered before Andra's mom could, "Can we talk privately?"

Raine stares, "Okay. We can talk in the den. Miss Coleman, can I get you and the baby something?"

Kim says, "Candy."

Miss Coleman laughs, "This girl is so spoiled. She saw that candy jar as soon as we walked in the door."

Raine laughed, "Help yourself, honey. Miss Coleman, the kitchen is right down that hall. You can help yourself to anything you want."

"Thank you, baby."

Raine and Renata walk into the den. Renata wasn't sure how she was going to handle explaining all of this to Raine, but she knew she had to try.

She turned and paused for a second, "Raine...we have a problem."

Raine stared as if she was confused.

"You see, these men are trying to kill LaJuan, and to get to her, they're trying to get her boyfriend and daughter..."

Raine was shocked, "Whoa, daughter? LaJuan has a child?" Raine nodded her head, "When did she have a child? I just saw her, and she never mentioned a child! Is that baby in there hers? That girl is something else...oh my God!"

"Calm down Raine, she didn't tell you because she was trying to protect Kim. If the people who are trying to kill her knew about the child, they would surely come after her. You've got to understand that, right?"

"Okay, I can get with that, but why do they want LaJuan dead? She's their star."

Renata took a deep breath, "LaJuan wants out. They found out that she was talking to a pastor about trying to get out of that organization. Now they want her dead. Personally, I never knew any of this stuff happened for real. I, like everyone else in the world, thought it was a rumor."

Raine sighed, "I know what she's feeling. I was there five years ago but in a slightly different way. Damien was abusing the hell out of me, and I was too young and dumb to do anything about it."

Renata said, "You weren't dumb, Raine. He just took advantage of your desire to be a star."

Raine continued, "Yeah, but Penny warned me. Everyone warned me, and I just wouldn't listen." Raine sat down in one of the chairs in the room, "I never told anyone this, but it all started in Damien's limo."

Renata said, "Raine, you don't have..."

Raine held up her hand to stop her, "I want to, Renata. In that limo, Damien told me that I wasn't cut out to be a star. He made me go down on him, and then he had sex with me. That's how I got the contract. I sold out to him."

Renata pled, "Raine..."

"No, Renata, some things you just have to get off your chest. I've never told anyone any of this, not even my closest friends. After I auditioned for the contract, Damien led me to the office. It was dark and scary. In there, they made me sign a contract...in blood. I should have run the hell out of there then, but I wanted it so bad. Nothing was going to stop me from getting that contract. Shortly after that, the abuse went from sexual to violent and mental."

Raine was crying, "He did it all to me, Renata, and they let him. As long as I was making money for them, they let him abuse me. He raped me weekly, and I couldn't say anything. He beat me almost every day, and I couldn't say anything. I hated my life everywhere but on stage. The stage was the only place I felt safe."

She paused, "So LaJuan probably only feels safe when she's out there on a mission, but now with the birth of her daughter, I'm willing to bet that she wants another life. Like me, she wants a better life, but I know as well as she does that they won't let it happen. They're going to kill her, or someone will have to pay the price for LaJuan."

Renata calmly said, "I don't believe that, Raine. She can repent and still be saved."

"You go on believing that if you want to, but the world me and LaJuan lived in doesn't work like that. Penny gave her life for me…LaJuan doesn't have anyone that would give their life for her."

Renata quietly sat next to Raine and put her arm around her, "Raine, you and LaJuan have been deceived. You see, our souls can't be sold to Satan, we are born into an unsaved world. When we find Jesus, we become saved. The reason these men want LaJuan dead so bad is because she's not saved yet! If she gives her life to Christ, they will have no power over her just as they had none over you. The power was in your belief that they had power over you."

Raine's tears were flowing down her face, "So my sister died for nothing?"

"No, sweetheart, we can't decide when our time comes. Your sister took that bullet for you because she probably believed that you were still trapped in a world of sin. As soon as you came back to church and asked God to forgive you, you became one of his children again. They couldn't stop that."

Raine jumped up, "Oh my God, LaJuan is out there thinking she has to die to be free."

"She doesn't need to die, Raine. The book of Acts says, 'Repent therefore and be converted, that your sins may be blotted out, so that times of refreshing may come from the presence of the Lord...'"

"How do you know all of this?"

"Raine girl, I've been studying for a long time. Before I even met Markus, I was in church, and my mom and I would always study together. Even today when I'm home, we'll have our little study sessions. The next man that comes into my life, he gone have to be saved!"

Raine laughed, "Amen, sister! So what do we need to do?"

Renata popped up rejuvenated, "Well, all I need you to do is take Kim and Miss Coleman to a safe place. I'm going to find Kyle and Andra. Then the three of us will try to find LaJuan. That's going to be hard."

Raine smirked, "Who you telling?"

Renata asked, "So you good?"

Raine answered, "Yeah, just don't tell anyone my story okay?"

Renata replied, "Raine, I'm a licensed counselor, and I hear stories all day. I don't tell any of them. I would never tell yours. You are my friend for life, so don't worry."

The explosion from the front of the house resounded so loudly that Renata thought her eardrums would explode. They both immediately fell to the floor, and Renata felt her heart racing.

She looked over at Raine, and she appeared to be unconscious. Renata heard shots and feared for Kim and Miss Coleman. She got up and tried to make her way to them. She was covered in dust. Before she left the room, she looked over at Raine one more time. She thought, *"God, I hope she's okay!"*

Renata got to the front of the house and heard Kim screaming. Renata yelled, "Let that baby go!"

Don smiled, "Well, look what we got here. Damn baby, you look as good as Raine."

He grabbed Renata's arm, "Let me go."

"Let me see...nope!" Don looked to his number one who was holding Kim like a sack of groceries, "Bring both of them. Now I know LaJuan will come to find us."

One of the men in suits asked, "What about Raine?"

"Where is she?"

Renata answered sternly, "She's dead. You killed her with that explosion!"

"Too bad, I really wanted that, but at least I got you to look forward to now."

Renata pulled away as hard as she could, "I'll never do anything with you!"

"Awww come on now, remember the child, you don't want her to be hurt, do you? You should come willingly to take care of her, or we'll have to do the best we can. Would you really trust me with a two-year-old?"

Renata couldn't resist and let them take Kim. She said through her teeth, "Give me the child."

The lieutenant handed Kim to Renata. Renata snatched Kim away from him and held her close to her body like a mother protecting her child.

Don said, "Now come with us, or things will get ugly."

Renata walked with them. She was terrified, but she couldn't let them take Kim by herself. She quietly prayed that Raine and Miss Coleman were still alive and would send help.

16

Raine was dazed. She barely made it to her feet. She looked around, and the house was in shambles. She was thankful that Jay and the kids weren't there, but she didn't see Renata or Kim anywhere.

She staggered around the room, and Renata and Kim were nowhere to be seen. She feared they had been taken. She suspected Don was behind it all.

She heard the sirens coming down the street as she continued to search the rest of the house for Renata, Miss Coleman, and Kim.

In the kitchen, she found Miss Coleman, but she was dead. Police officers and firemen filled the house.

"Ma'am, are you okay? Ma'am?"

Raine saw his lips moving but couldn't hear him. She panicked because she thought she had lost her hearing.

An EMT led Raine out the door and to an ambulance. Raine flopped down on the gurney and laid there. She started to cry because she knew Renata and Kim must be in Don's hands. Being the pervert he is, she knew that wouldn't be good for Renata. The ambulance made its way to the hospital as Raine quietly prayed for her friends. All of them needed God's protection.

***

Raine woke up in her hospital bed. A nurse was checking her vital signs. Raine asked, "How long have I been out?"

The nurse's face was covered with a facemask, but Raine could tell she was smiling, "You've only been out a few minutes, sweetheart."

Something was eerily familiar about that voice, those eyes. Raine wondered if she knew her, but the mask was blocking her face. The nurse looked at her and put her finger across her lips in a motion to keep Raine quiet.

She said, "Raine, I'm getting you out of here quietly before they realize you're still alive."

"Andra, is that you?"

She removed the mask, "Yeah, girl. I had that thing on, so they wouldn't recognize me. We heard about the bombing at your house and got there as soon as we could, but the ambulance had already left to bring you here."

"Andra, your mom...she's...well, she's..."

"I know. We saw them bring her out. Kyle is devastated. He also knows they have Kim and Renata."

Raine quickly rose, but her head started to pound. She dropped back down just as quickly. Andra laughed, "It's too soon for you to be trying to get up. Just let me wheel you out of here. Hold on."

Raine obeyed, knowing the price she'd pay for trying to get up again, "Okay, I promise not to move anymore."

They both smiled at each other. Raine and Andra met some years ago. Andra knew Raine as most people did. The Davis family was prominent in the area of Tampa, Florida, where they grew up. They immediately became friends through Renata. Now, Andra was helping to get Raine out of the hospital and to safety, but someone had to find LaJuan.

A doctor stopped Andra in the hallway, "Where are you taking this patient?"

Andra answered, "To X-ray."

The doctor was perplexed, "X-ray is in the opposite direction. Who are you? Take that mask off."

Andra replied, "I'm new."

The doctor reached for Andra's mask, and she swiped his hand away, stomped on his foot and turned to Raine, "Let's get out of here, girl!"

The pain didn't bother Raine this time, "I'm right behind you!"

They both ran out the exit door as the doctor was shouting behind them. They stopped in the parking lot where a van was waiting on them. Kyle asked, "I take it you had some issues."

Andra answered, "Some."

The van drove off, and Raine asked, "Why were we running?"

Andra answered, "Girl, we can't trust anyone. You of all people should know how these people are."

"You've got a point there." Raine sat back in her seat and prayed that Jay and her kids were alright. She asked, "Has anyone seen my husband and kids?"

Kyle answered, "I sent a secure message that couldn't be traced. I told him everything and advised him to get the kids and get out of town. We can only hope he did."

Raine replied, "Did he answer?"

"No."

No one said a word. Raine feared that her husband and her kids might be in danger as well. She only hoped that Don thought she was dead and would leave her family alone.

***

The doctor returned to his office and made a call, "Yes, this is Doctor Hakeem. She got away. Someone posed as a nurse and got her away from here."

All Doctor Hakeem heard was a "click." The phone went dead.

17

LaJuan pulled up in front of Raine's house. There were people still on the scene trying to figure out what caused the explosion. Police and fire personnel were everywhere.

LaJuan asked Raine earlier to follow the instructions in her Last Will and Testament if something happened to her, but now she feared that Don had gotten to the only person LaJuan called a friend. If Raine were dead, she would make sure Don died a slow horrible death. She clenched her teeth and tightened her jaws. She could think of nothing but revenge.

LaJuan saw Jay arriving on the scene with the kids. She could see the look of fear in his eyes. She got out the vehicle and ran over to him.

LaJuan said, "Jay."

Jay frowned, "Excuse me, I need to find my wife." He quickly glanced at her, "Don't I know you?"

LaJuan smiled, "No, but I know Raine, and she's told me about you."

Jay answered, "Yes…"

Jay walked up to a police officer and said, "I'm the owner, was anyone inside? What happened here?"

The officer replied, "You're the homeowner? You're Raine Davis' husband?"

"Yes sir."

The officer took him by the arm, "Okay." He motioned for a man in a suit and tie to come over." The man came over, and the officer said, "Sir, this is the Miss Davis' husband. Sir, this is FBI Agent Callahan."

They shook hands, and Jay asked, "Was my wife inside?"

Agent Callahan looked at LaJuan, and LaJuan quickly turned away, "She was, but she's okay. We sent her to the Melrose Memorial. The other lady didn't make it."

Jay was confused, "Other lady? There was someone else with her?"

"Yes, her driver's license said, 'Diane Coleman.' Did you know her?"

Jay answered, "No, I didn't." He turned to LaJuan, "Did you know her?"

LaJuan lied. She dared not say a word, and she didn't trust any man in a suit, even if he did say he was FBI.

Agent Callahan asked, "Who are you?"

LaJuan answered, "A friend of the family."

Jay said, "I need to go see my wife."

Agent Callahan replied, "Okay, but make sure you stay at the hospital, so we can ask you some questions."

Jay and LaJuan walked away. Jay asked, "You knew that woman, didn't you? I can tell by the expression on your face."

LaJuan answered, "Yes, I did. She's my daughter's grandmother."

"Why did you lie to the FBI."

LaJuan stopped, "It's a long story, Jay, but I'll suffice to say that Raine's life is in danger, and you have to get to her. I'm going to try and put an end to this myself but get to the hospital and to your wife. She needs you. Also, tell her she was the only friend I ever had."

"What?"

LaJuan walked off before Jay could ask any more questions. This had to end. She had to find Don and kill him once and for all. No one else needed to die.

Driving away, LaJuan thought about Kim. She was proud of the only good thing she had done in her life. She wanted Raine to know Kim. She wanted Kim to call her auntie or god momma. That was all in the Will that LaJuan left for Raine. She only hoped that everything would play out, so the two of them could know each other.

***

LaJuan was in front of Pastor Ponder's church. She thought, *"More police tape. Even a church isn't safe for these guys."* She slowly drove off.

It was fast becoming night, and she had no clue where to find her child, her boyfriend, and her friends. They had no skill to defend themselves, so she needed to be there to help them. She marveled at the thought that they were willing to put their lives on the line for her, but then she quickly changed it. She reasoned they were protecting Kim and really didn't care about her.

Raine might care somewhat about her, but after all she did to Raine, she didn't believe Raine cared so much that she would risk her life for her. She decided to call the hospital and see how she was doing.

She went to an internet café and decided to route her call through several IP addresses to make it harder to trace. LaJuan pulled over to an out-of-the-way café and went inside, carefully scoping out the scene to make sure no one was following her. She took a seat at one of the computers in the back of the store, again glancing around to ensure it was safe.

She kept her best friend on the seat next to her, never letting it out of her sight. This particular nine-millimeter had been with her for years and never let her down. She trusted it more than she trusted anyone in her life. It was loaded and ready for any situation.

She set up her last burner phone and routed the call through several IPs. Kyle had taught her some computer tricks. Now, they were coming in handy for her. *"It's truly the age of the geek,"* she thought.

Someone at the hospital answered, and LaJuan pretended to be Nya Davis and asked about her sister. The call was routed to someone else, "Hello, this is Mr. Swenson. You were asking about Miss Raine Davis?"

LaJuan answered, "Yes, this is her sister, Nya Davis."

"Yes, Miss Davis, I'm sorry, but your sister left the

hospital without telling us where she was going. Her husband is very distraught. Maybe you would like to talk to him?"

LaJuan hesitated but then responded, "Okay, thank you."

"Hey, Nya."

"Jay this isn't Nya. I was at the scene with you. Don't say anything, but I'm going to find Raine if it's the last thing on this Earth that I do. I promise you I will bring her back to you safely."

"Who are you?"

"LaJuan Craig." She didn't wait for an answer. She hung up the phone and logged out of the computer. She paid for her time and left the café on a mission. She didn't know what was going on, but her daughter, boyfriend, and best friend were in trouble. This had to stop, and it had to stop now. She was about to do the most dangerous thing she could possibly do in her life—take out the leader of the men in suits.

18

Raine was sitting in the van, thinking how her life had changed again. She was once a happy-go-lucky young woman, going to college and singing in her church choir. Then she was swept away in money, fame, domestic abuse, alcoholism, and drugs. Every day, she regretted the price for her fame. Her sister sacrificed her life to save her, and she would never forget it.

Now, she's still a famous singer, more famous than she ever was with Damien. She's a wife and mother. Things were great until this week. LaJuan comes back into her life, and everything goes crazy. She didn't know if she was going to live or die in the next few hours. Most of all, she didn't know how her husband and kids were doing.

She rode in the van, staring out of the window thinking, *"Will I ever escape this horrid life? Will the men in suits truly leave me alone? I hope Renata is right and that repentance is all LaJuan needs to do to escape."*

She watched all the people on the street going about their business. The night was taking over from the day, and she imagined most of them going on dates, meeting friends, enjoying family, or hitting the local clubs. She thought, *"None of them truly know the pain of this existence we live in. They don't know the evil that surrounds them each and every day. Satan is real, and he's busy deceiving anyone he can to get their soul. Thanks to my sister, I'm free, and God has me, but what about my friend? I need to convince LaJuan that she can and will be saved. I need to convince her that she needs to give her life to Christ. She doesn't have to die to be free."*

The vibration startled her. She reached in her purse and retrieved her phone. So much had transpired that she forgot she had it in her purse, "Hello."

"Hey, girl, where have you been? I've been calling and calling everywhere. I heard about the explosion at your house. You okay?"

"Yeah, I'm okay. I'm riding with Andra and her brother. We're trying to find LaJuan."

"Well, you know your big sister was worried about you. You could've called."

"I'm sorry, Nya. My head is spinning and everything. I'm just trying to get to a place where I'm safe."

Nya sighed, "Daddy took a turn for the worse."

"What? When?"

"A few hours ago. It seems whenever you're in danger something happens to him."

"Oh my God, Nya."

Nya said, "Look, you have to take care of your family out there. I'll take care of Daddy. Be safe, baby girl. Please be safe."

Raine paused, "I will, Nya. I love you. Tell Daddy I love him, too!"

Nya didn't respond. Raine asked, "Nya...are you there?"

Nya answered, "Yes, I'm here Raine. I love you too, and I'll tell Daddy you love him."

"Okay bye, Nya...kiss the kids for me."

"Bye, baby girl, and you do the same for me."

"I will." Raine pressed the disconnect button on her phone. A tear began to make its way down her face. It was happening all over again. She was in danger, and her father's health was fading. Nya was withdrawing into her quiet place.

Five years ago, Raine found herself in a very similar place. She wanted to go see about her dad, but she couldn't leave while LaJuan, Renata, and Kim were still missing. She didn't know what she was going to do. No one in the van knew the men in suits and Don like she did. She had to stay and help.

They pulled over to an abandoned warehouse and got out of the van. Andra asked Raine, "Are you okay? Did you get bad news?"

Raine answered, "Yeah, my dad's health has taken a turn for the worse. He was doing so well for the last five years, and now on today of all days, he has a relapse."

Andra comforted her, "We're here to pray for him and you, Raine."

Raine managed to smile, "I know. Thank you, guys, but we must find our friends."

Kyle said, "Let's go in here. I have some equipment stashed away. I'll set it up and see if we can track them down. Hopefully, Renata has her cell on her."

Andra added, "It was in her back pocket when she left us."

Kyle replied, "Yeah, let's hope it's still there."

Raine was quietly thinking about her dad and sister. She loved her family so much. She felt her phone vibrate again. Before she could answer, Kyle said, "You probably shouldn't answer that call. Your phone can be tracked just like we're trying to track Renata's. One call was enough, but a second one can surely lead them to us."

Raine replied, "Okay," and didn't answer the call. The ID said it was Jay. At least she knew he was still alive. That brought a smile to her face.

She followed behind Kyle and Andra, watching them move quickly to set up the equipment. Anyone on the outside would swear they were fully brother and sister. Raine knew, like most who knew them, that they shared the same father but different mothers. Andra never said anything about having a half-brother. To her, that was sacrilege. There was no such thing as "half" to Andra.

She admired Kyle and his intent to find his daughter. She knew his heart was heavy over the loss of his mother, but he kept it moving to find his daughter. Raine didn't know if he was motivated to find LaJuan, but Kim meant everything to him. He was one of the good dads in the world.

The equipment was all set up, and Kyle zoned into his world. Raine watched him work intently. She even smiled at how focused he became.

Andra said, "He gets into it, girl."

Raine laughed, "I see."

Kyle didn't utter a word as he kept pressing buttons on his computer. Raine just watched and prayed that he would find something that would lead them to his daughter and Renata. She couldn't imagine losing anyone else. She loved and admired Renata and prayed for her safety.

Kyle shouted, "Found her!"

The comment startled Raine and Andra. Raine held her hand over her heart, "Oh my God."

Kyle replied, "Sorry, Raine. They're on Washington Ave. near the Berkshire district."

Raine said, "They're probably at the Oasis Club. Damien and Don loved that lousy place."

Kyle picked up a bag, "Then that's where we're going."

They all headed to the van. Raine had grown increasingly nervous. What was she going to do when they got there? By no means was she a fighter. She hoped LaJuan would find them there as well. LaJuan would know what to do.

19

Nya hung up the phone call from Raine and slid down the hospital wall in tears. She couldn't tell her baby sister that their father had passed away. Raine had too much going on in California to be distracted by the news. It hurt Nya immensely to keep it from her, but there was nothing Raine could have done anyway.

Carlton helped his wife off the floor, and Nya cried on his shoulder. Nya felt the tender love of her children grasp her around her legs. Even in the midst of pain, their love healed.

Family and friends were there as well. Nya was glad for the support. She was always the strong one, but this time, she wasn't strong enough. She couldn't keep it inside, either. The hurt had to come out. It was coming out.

Six years ago, she lost her mother. A year later, she lost her sister, and now after five years of unexpected happiness, her father had gone home to glory. All that was left of the Davis family was her and Raine. If she were to lose Raine, she wouldn't be able to operate. She had to find a quiet spot and pray for Raine.

She looked Carlton in the eyes, "I need a place to pray."

"Okay, we'll go in that room."

"I need to be alone, baby."

Carlton held her tightly, "Where two or more, honey..."

"I know, but this time I just need to be alone...please?"

Carlton caressed her cheek, "Okay, go ahead. I'll be right here when you come out."

Nya quietly walked into the empty room. She knelt down and prayed, "Father, I love you so much, and I need you now. My family is almost gone. All I have left is my baby sister and she's...God, she's in danger. I know you already know what's going on with her. Please camp your angels around Raine, please protect my baby sister from all harm and danger."

Nya burst into tears, "She's all I got left, Jesus...please protect her, God. Give her the strength to save herself and her family. My brother-in-law, my nieces, and my nephew all need you, God. Father, I ask nothing for myself, but I ask everything for my sister and her family. If someone has to go, let it be me and not her. In your wonderful, powerful, and mighty son Jesus' name, amen."

Nya didn't move from that spot. Instead, she cried more and more. The loss of her father deeply affected her, and she knew it. That feeling of someone near crept into her spirit. The room was small, and she would have heard someone come in, but she didn't.

She looked up and gasped. She would bet her life that she saw her sister Penny. She knew it wasn't possible, but the vision was so comforting, she didn't want to let it go. She wondered, *"Is she telling me that Raine will be okay? God, I hope so! Thank you, Jesus!"*

Nya slowly rose and brushed herself off. In all her years, she learned that when God sends you a vision, believe it, have faith in it. Her mother often spoke of things God told her, and she trusted his word. Now, it was Nya's turn, and she would do as her mother did. She would trust the word of God.

She walked out of the small room and was greeted by her children. It was obvious that they were worried about her. She alleviated their worries and hugged them deeply. The oldest child asked, "Is Auntie Raine coming home?"

Nya smiled, "She sure is, baby. In a few days, you'll see your favorite auntie."

The children clapped, and Carlton put his arm around Nya. She knew all would be good.

20

LaJuan waited across the street from the headquarters building. Most people just assumed the building was another building like any other, but LaJuan knew better. This building was demonic, and she believed it housed the devil himself. If not him, then his right-hand. She thought, *"If he isn't the devil, he's close to it."*

She made it a point to learn the schedule of anyone who may one day become her prey. This man was no different. He was known as one of the richest men in the world. No one knew him or knew his face. He remained in the shadows, calling the shots and affecting the lives of so many people.

He had recruited her into a world of mysticism and death. She often thought of herself as death's angel. She didn't know how many people she had killed along the way, but she knew the time for killing had to end. It was going to end with the death of Kek Abaddon, the leader of the men in suits.

What little she knew of this man was derived from confidential files in the headquarters building. It is believed that he came from Iraq, but it has never been proven. No history of his childhood exists either. His wealth was amassed in the Middle East through oil purchases.

LaJuan knew this man controlled the world from this office building. Everyone worked for him, and no one dared challenge him. Don could not be coming for her unless he issued the order. If she were to capture or kill him, she could get the order recalled. Maybe even get her life back.

The moment came. He walked out of the building, and LaJuan was ready to act. She eased her weapon onto the steering column of her car and out of sight of anyone nearby. She cut the front windshield just small enough to put the barrel of the rifle through it. It was going to be a tough and uncomfortable shot, but it would allow her to speed off before his security team could gather themselves.

She was about to pull the trigger when the passenger side door swung open, and a man she didn't recognize got in, pointed a gun at her, and said, "I wouldn't do that if I were you."

She froze. She wondered, *"I must be losing my touch if I let this man get the drop on me."*

The man said, "If you pull that trigger, everyone in the world will be after you. There would be nowhere for you to hide. Do you really want that?"

LaJuan pulled the gun back, "I didn't plan on hiding. The only way out is death. If you know that man and me, then you know what I mean."

"I do know that man, and I do know who you are. As far as death being the only way out, well that I don't know, but we're working on that."

LaJuan looked coldly at the man, "Who are you?"

The man looked at LaJuan. His look was cold, but it was stern, and for one of the few times in her life, she was worried. She thought this was that moment when she would face death.

The man said, "My brother was killed five years ago, and I plan to get justice for his death."

LaJuan knew she was about to die. This was it, her time had come. A relative of one of her victims had now come to seek revenge. She managed to say, "You're Don's brother? He's alive."

The man looked away and then back at her, "No, I'm Jayden's brother. My name is Thomas McCall. Damien Black murdered my brother and his fiancé five years ago, but that man might as well have pulled the trigger. He's responsible for their deaths and the deaths of many others. I have tracked him and his organization for the last five years. That's how I found out about you."

LaJuan was relieved. Maybe she wasn't going to die today. She asked, "Why did you just save me?"

"Because killing him won't solve anything. We have to take down his organization. Dismantle it from the top down. Justice will do that, not killing him."

LaJuan smirked, "You're naive. That man will kill anyone who gets in his way. If he fears you have something on him, he'll have you eliminated. He's the closest thing to the devil himself. Hell, he might even be Satan."

Thomas smirked, "I'm naive? There's no such thing as Heaven or Hell, God or Satan."

LaJuan laughed, "I thought I was bad. At least I believe they exist. God doesn't care about me, but at least I believe he's there. You, you're out of your mind if you don't think the devil is alive and well, doing his 'kill, steal, and destroy' business. Heaven help you. Now get out my car. I have a devil to kill."

"Whatever our beliefs, we need to work together. That's the only way we can make this happen."

LaJuan pondered the thought. She never worked with anyone, and she didn't know this man at all. She remembered Raine telling her about Jayden. He was a good man who loved Penny. He died trying to save Penny from Damien, so if Thomas had the same or similar character, he could probably be trusted.

She said, "Okay, we'll try it your way, but remember, I'm a trained killer, and if I suspect a double cross, I won't hesitate to act."

Thomas smiled, "Never the trusting one, I accept your terms."

LaJuan put the rifle in the back seat, "What now?"

"We follow them and gather evidence. At some point, he will meet up with Don. That's when we should be able to get enough evidence to arrest him."

LaJuan stared in disbelief, "That's your plan? Really? Gather evidence and arrest him? That's not going to stop this organization. We need to kill them all, starting with Kek, then Don!"

"Hold on there…" LaJuan punched the gas, and the car shot off like a rocket.

Thomas shouted, "Stop you're going to get us all killed!"

"No, I'm going to kill him. You made me miss my opportunity!"

Thomas pointed his weapon at LaJuan, "Stop, or I swear I will shoot you."

LaJuan stopped the car, "I don't believe you. You'll shoot me and let that piece of garbage live?"

"I'm an officer of the law, and I don't go around killing people for a living. There's a way to take this organization down. You just have to trust me."

LaJuan really didn't know the meaning of trust. She slowly turned her head and looked at him, "What happens to my friends and my daughter in the meantime?"

"We'll save them. Just trust me."

"You'd better. I'm not the one you want hunting you down."

Thomas managed a smile, "That...I do know."

21

Renata sat quietly on the couch, holding Kim in her lap. She wasn't letting Kim go and even though Kim was asleep, she was holding onto Renata tightly. Renata knew she was scared, but she felt safe with Renata. That feeling kept Renata going. She wondered what it would be like to have her own children and hold them in her arms.

Quietly, she prayed that both of them would be safe from Don and his men. She didn't know Don personally, but she knew he had to be bad news if he was Damien Black's friend. The evil in his eyes scared her. She had nothing but the Lord.

In the next room, Renata heard shouting. It was Don shouting at someone on his phone. From what Renata heard, Don was angry because someone was telling him Raine was alive, and she got away from the hospital.

Renata smiled as Don walked into the room. Don sternly asked, "What are you smiling about? I still have you!"

Renata said, "You will never win. God will stop you and your evil ways. I believe in him, even if you don't."

"Oh, I believe in him alright. I just believe that he won't act when you think. You see, I got in on this years ago and everything I've wanted, I've enjoyed. Now I want you."

Don smiled. Renata felt dirty. She knew what he was thinking, and it made her angry.

One of Don's men walked into the room, holding a phone, "Don, it's him."

Don deeply sighed, "Yes." He paused listening, "Yes, I just found out she's alive, and she got away."

Don moved the phone away from his ear and then back, "Yes sir, I ordered them not to harm her. But sir..."

The phone apparently went dead, and Don appeared distraught. One of his men asked, "What do we do now?"

Don said, "Nothing. He wants to supervise things himself now."

The man said, "What do we do with them?"

Don sighed deeply, and as he walked away, he said, "We've been ordered not to touch either of them."

The man walked off, and Renata continued to sit there. She smiled heavily and praised God for saving her from

Don. She knew he answered her prayer. Kim was resting quietly through it all.

She lowered her head and closed her eyes. The warmth of Kim's little body made her feel comfortable and relaxed, but it wasn't long before the sound of guns blasting interrupted her relaxation.

Kim woke up screaming with fear. Renata did her best to keep her calm, but it wasn't working. There was a desk against the far wall. Renata carried Kim over to it and turned it on its side. She was amazed that she was able to do it with one hand. She thought, *"It must be the adrenaline in me!"*

Bullets continued to fire in the outer room. Renata prayed for their safety. She didn't know what was going on, but she hoped she was about to be saved.

Suddenly, it was silent. There were no sounds at all. Then she heard footsteps coming. She held Kim tightly and begged her in a whisper, "Don't make any noise okay, sweetie." Kim hugged her so tight Renata felt choked.

She heard the door slowly open and a voice, "I don't see anyone."

The voice ignited a reaction in Kim. She broke away from Renata and ran shouting, "Daddy! Daddy!"

Renata was happy they had found them. Raine and Andra hugged Renata, and they all felt a sigh of relief. Renata said, "Praise God you guys got here!"

Raine shouted, "Thank you, Jesus! I know how Don can be, so I was praying for you, girl."

Renata asked, "You were shooting, Raine?"

Raine answered, "Who me? No, girl, they did." Raine pointed to some men outside the room.

Renata asked, "Who are they?"

Raine answered, "A couple of them are my bodyguards, and the other ones are friends of Kyle."

Andra said, "Yeah, well that's all good, but the main one got away."

Renata frowned, "What? Don got away?"

Raine said, "Yeah, that coward scurried into the night."

Renata replied, "I felt like he was going to rape me, but someone called and stopped him. Thank God."

Raine responded, "Amen to that. Let's get out of here."

Kim ran back over to Renata smiling, "I love you!" She hugged Renata's leg tightly, and Renata couldn't hold back the smile if she tried. She picked Kim up and held her tightly as they walked.

Renata said, "I love you too, baby! I'm never going to let you go."

Raine added, "Aww, that's so sweet. They have a strong bond, Kyle."

Kyle was smiling, "Yeah, that's great..."

The bullet ripped the right side of his head to shreds, and Kyle's body slowly realized death had taken control. Everyone gasped in shock then hit the ground. Kim shouted, "Daddy!"

Renata refused to let her go this time, "No, baby, it's not safe!"

Kim kept shouting, "Daddy! Daddy! Daddy!"

More bullets rang out, and Renata saw two of the men that helped them go down. One of the remaining men ran to them, "Come on, we need to get out of here!"

Renata was holding Kim's face in her shoulder, so she couldn't see her dad. She didn't want Kim to remember him that way.

They ran out to a van where another man was waiting. Andra turned to Renata and Raine, "Get my niece to safety. I'm going to find Don and kill him myself."

Renata shouted, "No, you can't do that Andra! You're a model for God's sake, not a killer!"

"He killed my brother!"

Raine said, "Wait a minute. Here's what we need to do. Mel, you take Renata and the baby. Drive them out of town to a safe place somewhere. Renata, Mel is a saved man, and he can be trusted. I trust him with my life all the time."

Renata nodded her head as the tears came down her face.

Raine continued, "One of us needs to get that baby to safety, and she's grown attached to you, girl."

Renata said, "Okay, but what are you going to do?"

Raine answered, "Me, Andra, and Ty are going to find LaJuan. LaJuan is the only one capable of handling this situation. We can all dream of finding Don and doing something about him, but let's be real—she's the one that can actually do it."

Andra said, "Agreed. Take care of my niece, girl."

Renata replied, "I will." The three of them hugged each other tightly. Renata was praying that she would see her friends again.

She turned and got into the car with Mel. Kim waved bye to her aunt. Renata was amazed at how strongly Kim was attached to her, but she knew it was because of everything that happened that day.

She watched Raine and Andra jump in a van and drive off. Renata viciously rocked Kim, hoping she would fall asleep again, but she didn't. There was so much sadness in Renata's heart that she couldn't hear or think straight. She had only been this way once in her life. That was the day her boyfriend, Markus Black, died.

22

He stared out the office window of the Oasis Club marveling at his work. He owned over half the city of Los Angeles in some way or another. His corporate holdings were more than any man on Earth, but no one knew him.

No one knew the man who seemingly appeared from nowhere. Some say he came from Syria, while others say he came from Iraq. No one knew exactly, but he had become the most powerful man in the world.

He was the leader of the most powerful organization in the world. Many of its members were among the top 100 richest people in the world. Together, their fortunes controlled it all. Nothing was done without their input.

But on this evening, Kek Abaddgon was furious over the many failed attempts to end the life of LaJuan Craig. When LaJuan was brought into the fold, he was proud. He knew she had the talent to become the greatest assassin ever recruited. She lived up to that and more.

After she took care of Damien and the man she thought was Don, she began a downward spiral that led Kek to this moment. A moment where he now needed her dead.

Kek believed she was great as an assassin. She would be equally great as a Christian. He couldn't let that happen.

It broke his heart to find out that LaJuan secretly had a child. Then, she started talking to a pastor. That was the ultimate disrespect for him. No, she had to die, no matter what, she had to die. It had to happen before she decided to follow Christ. After all these years, Kek believed his lord and savior deserved to have LaJuan's soul. He worked hard to get it, and he couldn't allow it to slip from him.

He enjoyed the Oasis Club. It gave him peace to watch all the sin. Sure, there were some in the club whose souls he didn't completely have, but most of them were completely enveloped in sin. Those that weren't soon would be, as long as they stayed with his people instead of Christ.

He deeply sighed and waited for his lieutenant to join him in his office. Kek said angrily, "Don has failed us! LaJuan is still alive. The child is still alive, and now Raine has gotten involved."

The lieutenant calmly asked, "Do you really think she'll give her life to Christ?"

"We can't take that chance. She still believes our lies, but that may not last forever. If Don had succeeded earlier, we wouldn't have to worry. She must be eliminated now before she does. Find her. If you can't find her, then find her friends or that child."

"Why don't we eliminate them all?"

Kek leaned back in his chair, "We can't touch Raine Davis or her family. We also cannot touch Renata Smith."

"Yes sir."

The lieutenant left the room with his instructions. He didn't show any emotion at all, and Kek trusted him with his most important missions. Kek picked up the receiver and dialed a number.

"Hello."

"Don has outlived his purpose...eliminate him."

"Yes sir."

He calmly hung up the phone.

23

Don was out of breath after running from the warehouse where most of his team was now dead. He never expected Raine and her bodyguards to find them. Maybe he was so consumed with finding and killing LaJuan that he underestimated her. She was not the little girl that she used to be. She was much more.

This made him angry as well. As much as he lusted for her, he now wanted her dead also. He couldn't get Renata out of his head. She was elegant, intelligent, and beautiful. She had a spirit about her that attracted him. He couldn't stop thinking about her.

He would make it a point to find her and take her for his own. His cell rang, and it was one of his friends from the organization, "Hey dude, what's up?"

"Man, get out of town quick!"

"He gave the order?"

"Yeah, they're gonna find you and kill you."

"Damn, thanks, man. I'm getting out of here." Don hung up the phone, but before he did, he heard gunshots. He could only reason that his friend had been killed. He figured they knew he would tell Don, but he was thankful for the head start. Renata would have to wait. His life was more important.

He disposed of his phone. He didn't want to be tracked. Don found a parking lot and got a vehicle he could hotwire. He didn't know where he was going to hide out, but he had to find somewhere to go. They were going to track him until they killed him. They had eyes everywhere and knew his habits.

It was ironic that LaJuan would be the best person to help him in this situation, but she killed his twin brother, so she still needed to die. He reasoned that if he found LaJuan and killed her, the men in suits would forgive him and let him live.

He thought, *"Where would you be? If I were you looking for me, where would I go? Oasis! I would go to Oasis because you know that's my spot. I'm coming to kill you, LaJuan."*

***

He had to be careful around the Oasis Club. He wasn't the only one who liked to visit the club. He knew Kek liked to be there also, and most of his men would be there with orders to kill Don on sight. Don felt weird around Kek. He would love it when he saw the people drinking, cussing, or lusting after each other. He never understood why Kek got off on it so much, but he did.

Don found a good spot to hang out and scout the parking lot and surrounding area for any hint of LaJuan. He knew she would be near. She couldn't resist it. As good as she thought she was, Don felt he was better. He would kill her and be back in with the suits. It was that simple.

In the distance, Don saw a car pull up. He looked, but there were two people in it. LaJuan would never have a partner, so he dismissed that car and kept looking.

A group of ladies stood outside the club, and Don allowed his focus to switch to them. One of them was especially fine, and he let his thoughts float to her instead of where he needed to focus.

At the last second, he saw a gun pointed in his direction and ducked just in time. One of the two people in the car was LaJuan. He spun around and ran down the alley. The shots were coming at him, and he heard shouting behind him. Whoever the man was with her, he wasn't happy that she was shooting at him.

Don made it back to his car and sped off. No one appeared to be following him. He relaxed and laughed at how he was able to survive again.

24

LaJuan was visibly upset. She had him in her sights, and Thomas stopped her from killing him. She looked at him and shouted, "I warned you not to get in my way!"

"I warned you that I am an officer of the law, and I will not allow you to kill anyone in cold blood."

LaJuan looked him in the eye, "This partnership is over. You do things your way, and I'll do it my way. Just a word from one professional to another, stay out of my way."

Thomas said, "That's not the way to do things. We can catch them all together."

"Stay out of my way."

LaJuan walked off, leaving Thomas standing there. She never liked teaming up with anyone. Now that she missed killing Don, she hated having a partner even more.

She froze in her tracks when Kek's lieutenant stepped from the shadows. She suspected her life was now over. For the second time in one day, someone managed to get the drop on her. She was losing it.

The Lieutenant said, "Hello, LaJuan."

"Hello. I guess my time has finally come."

He smiled, and that scared LaJuan because she had never seen him smile before. He said, "Actually, no. I have a deal for you—you find Don and kill him. I'll put in a good word for you with Kek. You know my word goes far."

"A good word for me? He'll want me dead."

The Lieutenant replied, "You want him dead anyway, so even if you are to die, wouldn't you want it to happen after you've killed Don?"

He had a point. She wanted to see him dead, so why not take the deal. It would give her a little more time, and she could kill Don. She said, "Okay, I'll take your offer. Consider him dead."

"Excellent. You have 24 hours to complete your task or the deal is off."

She turned and walked off, "I won't need that much time."

***

LaJuan knew in the back of her mind that the Lieutenant didn't plan on keeping his word. After all, he worked for the richest man in the world who LaJuan believed was the devil. If only people had seen the things that she had seen, they would understand also.

Ten years ago, LaJuan was in Kek's office receiving instructions for her next mission. Suddenly, she was ordered to leave immediately. Before she did, she saw smoke rise up from out of nowhere. The room quickly grew extremely cold and eerie. LaJuan knew something evil was happening. She got out of there as soon as she could. She didn't ever want to go back.

There were dozens of instances where LaJuan suspected the organization was being run by demonic figures, but it was too late for her to be saved. She knew she couldn't get out of the organization, but if she could kill Don, it wouldn't matter. At least Kyle and Kim would be safe to live out their lives in peace. She could be a savior for them like Penny saved Raine.

She was on Don's trail. He didn't have many places to go now that the men in suits were after him. She would track him down and kill him in cold blood. She still didn't understand how she missed killing him five years ago, but this time, she would make sure he was dead.

There was one more spot that Don might go. The old Fresh City Records office building was a safe haven for him five years ago, and it probably would be now. After

Damien killed Penny and her fiancée, Fresh City got bad publicity. Raine was able to withdraw from her contract, which left Fresh City with no musical talent. In a year, they went under, and their offices and studios were left abandoned.

She hotwired a motorcycle and drove across town to Fresh City Records. She parked down the street from the office building and walked. She stayed close to the buildings to make it hard to see her coming. If Don were there, he'd be watching for her or anyone else.

She saw Damien's old apartment building across the street. She remembered how he used to take women there and abuse them. He tried the same trick with Raine, but it didn't work. Raine refused to go there, and that angered him to no end. LaJuan thought Raine would be different and not give in, but eventually, she did. Like all the others who wanted fame and fortune, Raine ended up selling her soul to get it. The difference here was Raine got out. Not many others could say that.

From a distance, LaJuan could see a car parked in front of the building. She suspected it was Don's. Across the street was another car. She didn't know who was in that car, but she suspected it might be the Lieutenant and his men.

LaJuan's senses were returning. She felt someone was near and placed her hand on her Glock. She was ready this time. If it were Don, he would die right now.

She waited until he was close. She swung around and raised her weapon in one swift movement. She pointed it at the head of the intended victim. She always took the head shot to ensure the kill.

"Wait!"

It was a good thing he spoke because she was ready to kill him, "What are you doing here? I told you we are not partners."

"I know what you said, but we still need to work together to end this for everyone. Killing Don will not end this. There is much more to do."

LaJuan said, "You're trying my patience."

Thomas calmly replied, "I'm trying to help you. I'm trying to help the world."

She took a deep breath, "I'm going in there. The only chance I have to live is if I kill him." She walked up to Thomas, "I know your law enforcement ethics don't allow you to do what I do, but they offered me a deal. One that I think they will go back on, but it's the only chance I have. He must die!"

Thomas stared at LaJuan. The thought crossed her mind that this man might have a crush on her. The look on his face was telling. She allowed herself to smile, then she saw something in the shadows. Something flashed in the darkness, and LaJuan quickly reacted.

She pulled Thomas down and fired five quick shots in the direction where the shots came from. She pulled Thomas behind the building while avoiding more shots. She returned fire.

The flashes were moving. Don was getting away again, but she couldn't go after him. Thomas was hit, and she couldn't leave him there to bleed to death. She hated her newfound feelings for people.

She realized her cold-blooded, uncaring nature was easing away. What was she turning into? A Christian? It couldn't be. A year ago, she would never have allowed her target to get away, but now she had to get help for Thomas.

She grabbed Thomas' phone and dialed 9-1-1 to report the shooting. In the distance, she heard Don's car start up and leave. She could still catch him if this woman would just take the information and send help for Thomas.

She wondered, *"What the hell is happening to me? Why do I care so much? I should just leave him and go after Don."* She looked at Thomas. He was a nice guy, a guy with honor and integrity. She respected him. *"I can't leave him to die alone."*

LaJuan hung up the phone. Help was on the way. She said, "Thomas, please don't die. You're one of the good guys. I'm not going anywhere until help comes, okay?"

He was breathing, but she got no response. She continued to talk to him until she could hear the sirens in the distance. When she could see the emergency vehicles, she moved away from the body. She couldn't get caught up in an investigation. She had work to do.

LaJuan hid in the shadows and waited until the paramedics started to attend to Thomas. She moved away and returned to her bike. She had no idea where Don would go now, but that wouldn't stop her. She would find him, and now, she had one more reason to kill him.

25

Raine and her bodyguard sat in the car, waiting on Andra to come back. She knew a friend who had a police scanner. They wanted to listen to the scanner for any hint of where LaJuan might be located. If there were any suspicious killings, they would suspect LaJuan would be near.

Raine was worried about everything. She missed Jay and the kids, and she knew they were worried about her. She wondered what was going on with her dad. She had no way of contacting any of them, so she just had to wait until this was over.

For five years, Raine had peace, and in a matter of a few days, her life was upside-down again. This was different than before. She wasn't the target of the abuse. LaJuan was being hunted, and they were just pawns being used to capture and kill her. The men in suits didn't care if they lived or died, but LaJuan had to die.

Raine's bodyguard received a call. He handed the phone to Raine. She asked, "Who is it?"

The bodyguard answered, "Renata."

Raine said, "Hey, girl. Isn't it dangerous for you to call?"

"My bodyguard said he didn't think so because he called your bodyguard. No one knows we're with them."

Raine replied, "Oh, I guess that's true. How are you and the baby?"

"We're good. He's taking us to a safe place, and we're swinging by to pick up Kyanna, Jay, and the kids also."

Raine smiled, "Praise God! Thank you so much for protecting my family."

Renata responded, "It's not a problem, my friend. I got you. Be careful out there."

Raine replied, "I will. Can you call Nya and see how my father is doing?"

"I'm sorry, Raine, but no one can call your family. They probably have those lines tapped."

Raine responded, "You're right. I'm just worried about my dad."

Renata said, "I know, Raine. We're praying, okay girl?"

Raine answered, "Okay. Be safe, Renata."

"I will. Take care, my friend."

Raine hung up the phone. She was happy that her family was safe, but she didn't know what was going on with her dad. She loved him so much and was grateful for the extra five years. If this was the end, then she couldn't complain.

She knew Nya would be devastated at the loss. She would be hurt, too, but Nya would take it worse. Their connection would have to be stronger than ever to get through it.

Andra jumped back into the vehicle with the scanner, "I got it, and there was a shooting by the old Fresh City Records building!"

"That has to be her."

Andra replied, "Yeah, and guess what…Jayden's brother, Thomas, was the victim. They're running him to the hospital."

Raine was shocked, "Why would she try and kill him? He's an FBI agent or something, right?"

"I don't know. Maybe he was trying to arrest her."

Raine said, "Okay, let's go to the hospital and see if we can talk to him."

Andra replied, "Good plan. Let's do it."

Raine smiled. She liked Andra. Neither of them knew anything about being an assassin or a spy, but they knew one thing—LaJuan had to be saved. Raine couldn't even understand why she cared so much. LaJuan did nothing but hurt her. Deep inside, Raine cared about anyone who wanted to change their life. Especially someone who wanted out of that organization.

26

LaJuan drove around the city streets, wondering where her target could have gone to hide out. For the last five years, she believed he was dead, so all of her information on him was outdated. She blew her chance at Oasis and Fresh City Records, so she had nothing else to rely on. She knew he wouldn't go back to the headquarters building because they wanted him dead now. All she could do was wander the streets and hope for a lead.

She turned down a popular street where two black sedans were waiting for her. She stopped, wondering if the men in suits had decided to take her out before she could kill Don. Kek stepped out of one of the sedans and adjusted his suit. LaJuan thought, *"This must be important."*

She got off her bike and walked within three feet of Kek. She made sure her gun was ready. She may not live, but she was going to take someone with her.

Kek gave his deceiving smile, "Good evening, pretty lady."

"Kek."

He took two steps towards her and stopped, "It's always pleasant to see such a beautiful lady like you."

She sighed deeply, "Can we stop with the BS? Are you here to kill me or what?"

"So cold. You were my best until you had to go out and have that bastard child."

LaJuan wanted to cut his throat. She secretly despised him, but for some reason, he seemed to like her. Now, he was calling her child a bastard. She hoped she would live long enough to kill him.

"Can you get to the point? Either you're going to kill me or let me do my job."

Kek continued to smile, "Oh, we have a few minutes before you can get to work. Aren't you the least bit curious as to how Don managed to survive your gunshot to the head? I mean really, how could he?"

She was intrigued. How did he survive? She decided to play along, "Okay, how did he?"

Kek folded his arms, "We have the power even over life and death itself. You see, you want to leave an organization that can bring you back to life. Why would you give that power away? We can offer you so much that this world can't offer you."

"You can't give me a nice quiet life with a husband and my child, can you? No, you can't. You can only give me a life of killing. As long as I kill for you, I can live. My child will not know that life. You won't get your hands on her. I'd rather die than let that happen."

Kek smiled vanished, "You disappoint me, LaJuan." He returned to his sedan, "1424 Langston Hughes Drive, that's where you'll find your target. See that he's dead before sunrise."

LaJuan shouted, "The deal?"

Kek smiled. LaJuan knew they weren't going to keep the deal. She knew she was going to have to kill him, too. She thought, *"So be it. I'll kill you too."*

She got back on her bike and headed towards the address. She would kill Don and devise a plan to kill Kek. She knew she would have to have help to do it. She really needed Thomas to back her up, but she knew even if he were there, he wouldn't do it. His integrity wouldn't allow it.

As she rolled through the city streets, she dreamed of a different life. She dreamed of a life with Kyle and Kim. She laughed picturing herself as a soccer mom, carting the kids around to practice and games.

She wondered if her kids and Raine's kids would be friends. That would be perfect for her, but then she dismissed the thought. Her choices would be the death of her. She couldn't escape it. The blood contract meant she sold her soul to the devil, and there was no coming back from that. Unlike Raine, she didn't have anyone who would make the ultimate sacrifice for her. She would have to make that sacrifice for Kyle and Kim.

She made up in her mind that she would kill Don and make every attempt to kill Kek. If she died trying to kill him, then so be it. Her child would be safe with her dad.

She pulled up to the house. There were no lights on inside, but the car that was at Fresh City was in the driveway. She checked her Glock as she always did before a kill It was loaded and ready.

She eased up to the house and went around back. It was a one-story building. She was able to peek through one of the windows and saw Don on the couch with a woman. LaJuan wanted to puke. She remembered having slept with Don five years ago just to keep informed on Damien's business. She hated him then, and now she hated him even more.

She didn't recognize the woman, so she must have been new to the game. Unfortunately, she was in the wrong place at the wrong time.

LaJuan went around to the back door and quietly forced her way inside. She was a master at breaking and entering as quietly as a church mouse. She eased her way towards the room where Don and the woman were. They weren't kissing anymore, they were talking, and she could hear them.

The woman said, "I can't believe you killed someone."

Don replied, "I had to, he was going to kill me."

LaJuan stopped. She wondered, *"Who is he talking about...Thomas? He's dead?"*

The woman continued, "But why would a computer guy want to kill you? Kyle was a nice man, he never seemed like the type to hurt anyone."

LaJuan was furious. She took a deep breath pounced into the room, "You killed him!"

Don jumped up and looked at his weapon on the far side of the room. LaJuan continued, "Try for it, I dare you!" She was so angry, "You killed my boyfriend. Now, I'm gonna kill her!"

The woman shouted, "No, please don't."

LaJuan aimed the gun at the woman, but Don didn't say anything. It was as if he wanted her to kill the woman. Something wasn't right.

She said, "You want me to kill her. Why...why do you want me to kill this woman?" She pointed the gun at Don.

Don said, "You've gone soft. Years ago, you would have just killed her and then me. Now you wait. What, you got a conscience now?" He looked at his gun.

"Not enough of one that would prevent me from killing you. Go for that gun, so I can kill you now."

The woman said, "You want her to kill me because you know my death will damn her to Hell."

LaJuan asked, "What are you talking about?"

The woman continued, "You know the story of Job where Satan has to ask permission to harm Job?"

"Somewhat...maybe...what's that got to do with anything?"

The woman said, "Five years ago, Damien killed Penny Davis. The Illuminati was told not to harm any member of the Davis family. When Damien killed Penny, he was damned to Hell. You know because you were there." She turned to Don and said coldly, "You were using me. You wanted her to kill me, so she would have the same fate as Damien."

"I had to try, didn't I? She killed my brother!"

LaJuan was confused, "Your brother? You're protected? I don't know what the heck is going on here, but one thing I do know is that you're not protected." She pulled the trigger and shot Don in the stomach.

He fell to his knees and gasped, "What, no head shot?"

"No, I want you to suffer. You killed my boyfriend, the father of my child. Now, I want you to slowly die."

The woman said, "I'm calling an ambulance."

LaJuan turned to her, "No, let him die, he needs to die."

"I can't just let a man die."

LaJuan turned to Don, "It would've been fun to watch!" She put two more bullets into Don. The first hit him in the chest, the second in the head. He was dead.

She looked at the woman, "Now, you don't have to hurry and call anyone." LaJuan put her weapon away, "What did he mean by brother?"

The woman was in shock, "Ummm...Don had a twin. The woman who you thought he was seeing was seeing his twin. I know because I was that woman. Darryl was at my apartment the night you killed him. I don't hold any anger towards you because I gave my life to Christ the next year. You see, your killing him changed my life. You could say that it saved my life. I now work with battered and abused women at a shelter. I know I'm protected because Don told me his boss said to get you to kill me. If you did, you'd be damned to Hell. You wouldn't have a chance to be saved."

LaJuan said, "I still don't have a chance. Your God...he hates me."

She turned and walked out of the house as the police sirens came quickly down the street. Her mission was over, she had killed the man who killed her boyfriend and tried to kill her. Now, she had to go after the man in charge. She had to kill Kek or die trying. Either way, her daughter would know happiness forever.

27

Raine was chosen to slip inside the hospital and find Thomas. She was most familiar with him, but she was also the most known. She had to disguise herself. On the way to the hospital, they stopped at one of Andra's makeup artist's apartment. Raine grabbed a blonde wig and put on some makeup.

Inside the hospital, she put on a nurse's outfit and found a clipboard. She went to Thomas' room, but police were in the room asking him questions. Raine had to wait to get in there and see him.

After a few minutes, the police and agents left, and Raine slipped into the room. Thomas was still awake. She asked, "Hi, Thomas, do you remember me?"

Thomas stared, "Well, ahhh..."

Raine removed her wig and said, "How about now?"

Thomas smiled, "Raine? Raine Davis, is that you?"

"Yeah, it's me. How you doing?"

Thomas tried to sit up, "I've been better. What are you doing here dressed like that?"

"I'm trying to find my friend LaJuan Craig. Was she with you?"

Thomas said, "Yes she was, and I think I had her convinced not to kill Don or Kek, but now I fear all of that is out the window. She's probably either killed one or both of them."

Raine dropped her head, "Oh no."

"'Oh no' is right. If LaJuan goes after Kek, she'll be killed."

Raine asked, "Do you know where she is now?"

"I have no idea, but you can bet she'll go after Kek. Wherever he is, that's where she'll be."

That was something Raine didn't want to hear. She didn't want to go anywhere near Kek or anyone in the organization again, but she had to help LaJuan. It was the greatest sacrifice she would make today. She had to be strong and do this.

Raine said, "Okay thanks, Thomas. Pray for us."

"I will, Raine. I would tell you not to do it, but I know from my brother that you won't listen."

Raine smiled, "Your brother was a smart man and knew me well. Bye, Thomas."

"Bye, Raine."

***

Raine sat in the vehicle with Andra and the bodyguard. She didn't say anything at first, pondering the thought of seeing Kek again. Andra asked, "Well, what did he say? Don't keep us in suspense."

Raine answered, "Oh, I'm sorry. I was just thinking about something."

Andra said, "Okay, so what did he say?"

Raine replied, "He thinks LaJuan is going to kill Don, which we expected, but he thinks she's going after the leader of the men in suits. She has a death wish. She'll never get to him."

Andra responded, "She probably thinks that's the only way out of the organization. She either kills him, or she dies."

Raine replied, "Even if in some imaginary world she does kill him, she'll still die. They will kill her. She doesn't understand that to take these guys down, you have to do it in courts or on a platform. Killing Kek will only have him replaced by someone else...or something else."

"Something else?"

"Never mind, we need to go camp out at the headquarters building. She'll probably wait for him there."

"But Raine, it's only 3am. He'll get in this early?"

"No, he won't, but she'll camp there all night if she has to. This is LaJuan Craig we're talking about."

Andra smacked her lips, "True."

28

LaJuan was on her bike about a mile away from where she killed Don. Thoughts raced across her mind. The men in suits wanted her to go after Don to not only kill him but to kill one of God's protected, so her fate would be the same as Damien's. Kind of ironic, she thought. She knew they would never honor the deal, and now she had proof.

She was so deep into her thoughts. She didn't hear the sound of the shot until it pierced her shoulder, knocking her off the bike instantly. They had followed her, and now they were trying to terminate her.

Shots were ringing out from everywhere. LaJuan rolled under a nearby car and removed her Glock. She didn't know what direction the shot came from. They wounded her shooting shoulder. It would be hard for her to shoot with the opposite hand, but she had no choice.

The shots continued to ring down on her position until police sirens began heading her way. She knew the men in suits wouldn't chance staying there. They worked in the shadows, not exposing themselves. She waited until it was safe and crawled from underneath the car.

LaJuan managed to get her bike up with her good arm and get on it. She rode away, needing to find a place to attend to her wound.

***

She didn't know how far she had driven, but she was getting weak. She was losing blood and consciousness quickly. She lost control of the bike and fell in the street. She hoped that the men in suits weren't near. She was an easy target. Her eyes were slowly closing. She saw someone running towards her, but she couldn't move. She couldn't defend herself. She figured she was soon to be dead.

***

LaJuan struggled to open her eyes. Her blurred vision made it difficult to make out the person standing next to her. She said, "Hell isn't so bad. It doesn't even feel hot here."

She heard laughter then a familiar voice, "Honey, this is not Hell at all. Welcome back."

"Raine? Is that you?"

Raine was smiling, "Yeah baby, it's me. We found you lying in the street half dead."

LaJuan tried to get up, but Raine gently guided her back down. LaJuan said, "I can't be in a hospital, they'll find me here."

An unfamiliar voice said, "You're not in a hospital hun, you're in my home. I'm a doctor, and you aren't strong enough to move right now."

Raine said, "LaJuan, this is Doctor Trina Washington. We've been friends since...forever. She treats me, and this house is not in my routine at all, so no one will know you're here."

LaJuan relaxed somewhat, "Okay. What's in the IV?"

Doctor Washington answered, "Just giving you some intravenous fluids and morphine for the pain."

LaJuan reached for the IV, "No, no drugs!"

Doctor Washington said, "Hold on hun, you need the morphine. No one can take that pain."

LaJuan shouted, "Take it out...now!"

Raine said, "Do it, Trina. She's not normal."

Doctor Washington removed the IV drip, "You still need fluids to hydrate your body."

LaJuan replied, "Give me some water but no meds. I need a clear head for what I'm about to do."

Raine was looking pitiful, "You can't do it, LaJuan. Kek is too powerful to go after. Just walk away."

"He is responsible for killing Kyle. I'm getting my revenge, or I'll die trying."

Raine plead, "It doesn't have to be that way, LaJuan."

"It does for me, Raine. Just leave it alone, and please don't start with the 'God loves even you' crap. Today of all days proves that God doesn't give a damn about me."

Raine nodded her head, "That's just not true. LaJuan, look, the men in suits...well, their greatest strength is the power to make you believe that you have no hope."

"Please, Raine, stop! I don't want to hear it. I just need some rest, and then I'm going to kill Kek. Where's my baby?"

Raine sighed, "She's with Renata. The two of them have formed a serious bond together. Kim wouldn't let her go."

LaJuan smiled, "That's good to know. Do you think she'll make a good mom?"

"Renata? Hell yes! Almost as good as me."

LaJuan chuckled, "You are the most conceited person I know, but I love you, Raine. If I don't make it through all of this, make sure my child is cared for. I don't care if it's you or Renata, just make sure she's okay. Please?"

Raine said, "First of all, I'm not conceited. Second, you're going to make it through this, okay?"

"Raine please, promise me?"

"Okay, LaJuan, Kim will be well taken care of by one of us. Right now, I'd have to say that's going to be Renata because of their bond, but I will keep myself in the loop and make sure she's good. But...you're going to make it. Trust me, God has you."

"Spare me. I need some rest, Raine."

"Good night my friend, but I'm not giving up on you. I'm still praying for you."

LaJuan decided not to respond. As much as she believed that God didn't care for her, Raine believed he did. The two were not going to agree anytime soon. At that moment between sleep and consciousness, LaJuan saw a figure motioning to her to come to him. She didn't understand it. She could see him, but then again, she didn't. It was like he existed, but he didn't. He was wearing a crown, and his skin was like bronze. What she did know was that his presence calmed her spirit, and she fell asleep without any worries.

***

LaJuan woke up. She didn't know how long she had been asleep. No one was in the room, so she decided to try and get up. The immense pain in her shoulder assured her that Doctor Washington didn't give her any drugs. She staggered to her feet and grabbed her blouse. She almost had it on when Raine came in to help.

Raine was frustrated, "Girl, what are you doing?"

"Thanks, Raine, but I have work to do. I can't stay here forever."

"LaJuan, you can't do this."

LaJuan worked to manage a smile, "I have to, Raine. You don't fully understand. You spent six months with these guys, I've been in the organization for over 20 years. Trust me when I say, I have seen things you wouldn't understand. I have to do this."

Raine welled up, "LaJuan..."

"Raine...please stop. I love you girl, but I can't do it your way. What does the Bible say about faith...a mustard seed or some crap like that? I don't even have that much faith. I have to do it my way."

Raine didn't respond. She just looked at LaJuan. LaJuan couldn't look her in the eyes. After all they had been through, it came down to this day. They both knew they loved each other. She only hoped they would be friends again.

"I'll still be praying for you, LaJuan. I love you."

LaJuan smiled, "Thanks. I can use the help."

LaJuan hugged Raine, figuring it to be the last time they hugged. She realized it was almost evening again. She had slept all day. Around this time, Kek would probably be at the Oasis Club eating dinner. That's where the final showdown would happen. She would meet her fate at the Oasis Club.

$$***$$

Before she went to the showdown with Kek, LaJuan had to make a stop. She met Wayne Bivins when she needed help filling a contract. Wayne was the best of the best.

She pulled up to an old warehouse building that appeared to be abandoned. LaJuan knew it wasn't. She tapped out the code to the inconspicuous side door and went in. She had been to this building many times before. She walked to the dimly lit office.

"Took you long enough. I started to think you weren't going to make it."

"I got sidetracked."

"Looks like you got shot. Who's that good?"

"It's not important. You got the stuff ready?"

The tall man stood from behind the desk and stared at LaJuan, "Yeah, I got it." He led her to the next room.

LaJuan looked over the items lying on the table, "This everything?"

"You know I wouldn't cross you."

"I know." She paused, "Look, this might be our last time speaking. If it is, know that I think highly of you and your work. There's none better."

Wayne said, "Let's just hope it's not."

LaJuan nodded, "Here's the cash. Hook me up."

Wayne didn't bother to count it. There was unspeakable respect between them. LaJuan wouldn't have counted any money from Wayne either.

After 30 minutes, LaJuan was ready to head out. Wayne asked, "Got time for a drink?"

LaJuan smiled, "With you, sure."

Wayne grabbed the bottle, "I save the best for you."

"Let me guess, bourbon, right?"

"You got it. My father used to say, 'If you ain't drinking bourbon, you ain't drinking.'"

"You say that every time, Wayne."

They tap glasses and drink, "Yeah I know, but it's always appropriate."

"True. Thanks for the drink, my friend. See you around."

"I hope so, LaJuan, I truly hope so. Take care."

LaJuan walked away without looking back. She knew Wayne was watching her, but she didn't want the moment to linger. She expected to die, and she knew Wayne was the only connection that would honestly miss her. Everyone else was just business. Wayne was like a big brother.

***

LaJuan had to make one more stop before the showdown. She pulled up to her customary parking slot. Only one car was in the parking lot. He greeted her as soon as she got out the car.

"How are you, my sister?"

"I'm good, Pastor. I'm sorry about Channel."

"It's not your fault. So, what brings you here at this late hour?" He tossed his keys on the desk, turned, and smiled at LaJuan."

LaJuan thought about her decision. It didn't come easy, but she decided no matter what, she had to try, "Well, Pastor, I think it's time."

"Let me understand correctly, you want to give your life to Christ?"

LaJuan took a deep breath, "Yes."

Pastor Ponder put his arms on LaJuan's shoulders, "Let's do this."

29

The Oasis Club often held dinners for the richest men in the world, and this was one of those evenings. Several of the world's most powerful men gathered for dinner with their leader. This was supposed to be a meeting to celebrate the election of a new leader in one of the countries of the European Union, but instead, there was growing concern over the mishandling of LaJuan Craig.

The most vocal of the group's members was a man from Germany named Keil Manheim. Keil was thought to be the next leader of the group. He was vocal and outspoken over any issue that didn't look good for the group. Recently, he criticized moves that Kek had made, especially those relating to LaJuan. He believed that LaJuan should have been taken out by a specialist and not by Don.

Kek stood up at the table, "Gentlemen, we are here to celebrate the growth of our power in the EU. Moves that we started as long as eight years ago are now coming to fruition. In the coming years, we will be able to control approximately 82 percent of the world's oil reserves. Couple that with our holdings on the world's food reserve, and we're in prime position to control the world."

Kek paced around the table. He knew there was opposition to his rule. It was not unfamiliar territory for him. There had been challenges to his leadership before, and those men mysteriously disappeared. However, he had to publicly do something this time. Keil was challenging him, and it had to stop.

He pointed to the map on the wall, "This map shows how powerful our hold on the world will be in approximately two years. When this world's food supply begins to drain, we will be in control. We will determine who eats and who doesn't. Countries like the United States will bow to us. Millions will starve, but those that believe in our one religion will be fed. Those that wear the mark will eat."

Keil slammed his fist on the table, "Everyone knows all of that! Hell, we've known for years that we would be situated as we are. The Bible even tells us that we would be here." Keil moved from his seat, unbuttoned his jacket, and stood before the members. He continued, "Our problem isn't oil or food but LaJuan Craig! She was a vital member of this organization, and now we are on the verge of losing her because our incompetent leadership has allowed her to escape."

Kek took his seat. He was furious inside, but he couldn't show his rage in front of the membership and not in

Oasis. Oasis was a safe haven, but he planned to deal with Keil. He had to stop him. This was not going to go without a response.

Kek asked calmly, "What do you suggest we do, Mr. Manheim?"

"We find her, and we kill her. It's that simple."

Kek said, "That is being done. LaJuan has done exactly as I have orchestrated. She failed to kill the protected one, but she did eliminate Don for us. He, too, was becoming a problem. Now in a few hours, LaJuan will be eliminated. Give it time. As with all things run by this organization, patience is the key."

Keil readjusted his jacket and took his seat. Kek had thwarted his attack for now, but LaJuan would have to be dealt with soon. He knew LaJuan would come after him because of the failed attempt on her life. It was only a matter of time.

***

Kek went into the next room to take a call. The room was on a high from the news that the Biblical prophecies were coming true, and they would rule the world. Kek stood in the center of the next room, "Hello."

"Sir, we have not located her, but we have everyone on this."

Kek explained, "You do not need to look for her. She will find us. You can assure yourself that wherever I am, she will be. Bring all your men here and position them around the club. Do not allow her to escape."

"Yes sir."

"I also have another mission for you. When Keil Manheim leaves the club tonight, he is to have an accident. It needs to be public and blamed on a terrorist group. It can have nothing to do with this organization or me. Is that clear?"

"Yes sir, we will take care of it. We anticipated this problem and people are in place and ready."

"Good." He hung up the phone and returned to the room where the men in suits continued to eat and celebrate.

***

It was after midnight, and the meeting was ending. Most of the men in suits were heading off with dates provided by Kek. It was a tradition that Kek would provide female entertainment for them on their visit, and this wasn't any different. However, he ensured that the woman Keil left with was loyal to him and would direct Keil and his entourage in the direction Kek wanted him to go. He needed Keil to die at the hands of someone not affiliated with the organization, and it had to happen tonight.

Kek's computer personnel tapped into the city's street camera system, so Kek could watch Keil's motorcade. It was headed in the path orchestrated by Kek. His operative had followed instructions perfectly, but he knew she would. She was perfect for the job, and Kek would ensure she would be rewarded. She would no longer have to work at these parties.

He watched as mercenaries assaulted the motorcade in front and back. They pulled everyone out of the vehicle and gunned them down. The last two were Keil and Kek's operative, Vivian.

Kek called Keil's number, "Hello, my friend. It appears that you have a situation. Do you need my assistance?"

"Kek, you bastard, I know you're behind this! You're going to pay."

Kek laughed, "Really...you're even arrogant when facing sure death. Goodbye, my friend, and say hello to our master."

The mercenaries gunned him down and then aimed the guns at Vivian. She shouted, "I'm with Kek, we made a deal!"

One of the mercenaries handed her the phone, "Kek, tell them we have a deal!"

"Yes, my dear, we do have a deal. In return for setting Keil up, you will never have to work at the parties again. I gave you my promise, and I will keep it. Hand the phone to him."

She handed the phone to one of the mercenaries. Kek said, "Kill her."

The mercenaries didn't ask any questions. He shot Vivian in the head, killing her instantly. Kek hung up the phone and reared back in his seat. He punched the intercom, calling his IT manager.

The manager answered the intercom, "Yes sir."

"Make sure all the footage is destroyed. No one can see what truly happened."

"Yes sir."

Kek was proud of himself. He had successfully eliminated another rival, and if all went well with the cleanup, it wouldn't trace back to him. No one could stand in his way. Yes, the organization would rule the world, but he ruled the organization. Therefore, he would rule the world.

30

The rain fell gently on her face as she stood in the shadows. She was across the street from the building she considered evil. She didn't even desire to wipe it away because it felt like she was being cleansed. As he would do every morning, Kek would soon return to this location and start business as usual. She was doing her business as well. For one of them, it would end. One of them would die this morning, and she was prepared to handle it either way.

LaJuan's thoughts were on her task, but she couldn't help but wonder how her daughter was doing. She knew Kim was in good hands with Renata, and she was pleased to hear that she had formed a bond with her. Renata was a good, upstanding woman who LaJuan knew could be trusted. She didn't have a trace of evil within her. She would make a good mother to Kim. If LaJuan had to die, at least she would do it knowing her daughter was in good hands.

She also thought of her one and only true friend Raine Davis. She wondered what Raine was up to since she left them. She knew Raine wasn't the type to leave things alone. She only hoped that she wouldn't be crazy enough to come down here. She didn't want her to get in the crossfire.

Raine had been freed from the evil organization they often referred to as "the men in suits." Some people knew their true name while others only believed they were a myth. LaJuan knew the truth. She knew who they were and what they stood for, and that was reason enough to kill her. If she was planning on leaving the organization, they had to kill her. No one just left the group.

Mysterious deaths of high profile people were common. People thought it was a car wreck or a drug overdose. In reality, a lot of the work was LaJuan's. She was the best at making a scene look like an accident, but now they were after her. She wouldn't go down without a fight.

She continued to wait in the morning shadows directly across from the building. When Kek arrived, she would put a bullet in him as soon as he got out of his expensive limo. Then, she would deal with the bodyguards. She didn't care what happened to her after that because her mission would be complete.

However, her plan took a turn for the worse when another car pulled up seconds before Kek's vehicle. LaJuan stomped her foot to the ground and fell back against the wall, "Damn it, Raine!"

She knew Raine wouldn't leave it alone, and now here she was interfering with LaJuan's mission. She mumbled, *"Raine, you can work a sister's nerves."* Now, she had to adjust. She couldn't let anything happen to Raine. The mere thought of caring about another person let LaJuan know she had changed, but she didn't have time to think about that. She had to come up with a new plan, one that protected her only friend from any harm.

She moved to a higher vantage point, but she knew she couldn't fire on Kek because Raine could get hit by a stray bullet. She had to watch and hope for an opening.

Kek stepped out of his limo, and Raine greeted him. LaJuan was furious. It would have been the perfect shot. She could have easily killed him and probably gotten away. She mumbled, *"Raine what are you doing?"*

Raine and Kek walked inside the building. She didn't think Raine would ever go in that building again, but there she was going inside. If she had any doubts before, they were gone now. Raine Davis loved LaJuan like a sister.

LaJuan turned and sat with her back to the wall, *"What am I going to do? I need to get inside that building, but I know that's just about impossible. Raine, why did you do this? Ugghhh, she can get under my skin sometimes, but I love my sister."*

LaJuan looked back on the street. From a distance, she could see one of the secretaries with top floor access coming towards the building. If she moved fast enough, she could cut her off and take her credentials. Then, she could disguise herself and have a chance to get into the building to save Raine.

She quickly left her vantage point and went after the secretary. LaJuan came up from behind the woman, and with one quick motion, she subdued her and pulled her in a nearby alley.

LaJuan removed the woman's credentials and put the lanyard around her neck. Fortune was smiling on LaJuan because the lady had on a wig. LaJuan removed the wig and placed it on her head. She looked in a mirror and smiled, *"I look good as a redhead."*

LaJuan used some of the makeup to help with her disguise and put shades on to cover more of her face. When she was done, she headed out to the street and then to the building.

Once on the street, LaJuan's heart dropped. She said softly, *"Raine."*

Kek and his men were taking Raine out of the building toward his limo. This wasn't good. LaJuan removed her Glock, threw off the wig, and ran toward them.

The men in suits saw her and pointed their guns at her. Raine shouted, "LaJuan, run!"

LaJuan couldn't run and leave her friend. She dove behind a car, and the pain from her bullet wound escalated. She thought, *"I wish I had that morphine now."*

Kek yelled, "Throw your weapon out and come out, LaJuan Craig, or Raine will breathe her last breath."

LaJuan hit her head against the car, cursing Raine under her breath, *"Why did you have to come here!"*

Kek continued, "I'll give you ten seconds, then I must kill her."

"You can't kill her, it's against the rules!"

He laughed, "Do you want to test that theory?"

LaJuan tossed her weapon on the sidewalk. She pulled out her cell and punched in 9-1-1. She dropped the phone, knowing the police would trace it and come to her location. She stood up and walked out. Kek was holding Raine by the neck, and fear was all over her face. No matter what happened to her, she couldn't let Raine die.

Kek smiled, "Well, well, well, it comes down to this...me and you, like the O.K. Corral."

LaJuan smirked and nodded her head, "Let her go and give me my weapon, then we'll be like the O.K. Corral."

"You must take me for a fool, LaJuan. I had you trained to be the best in the business. If you hadn't turned on me, you still would be the best."

LaJuan said, "Let her go, and I'll consent to anything you want, just don't hurt my friend."

Kek laughed, "Wow, you really have changed. You, LaJuan Craig, showing concern for another human being? That baby must have changed you more than I know. I wouldn't believe it if I didn't hear it for myself."

LaJuan said sternly, "Let her go, Kek, the police will be here soon, and everyone will see you."

Kek got very serious, "You forget I own the police, the FBI, the CIA, and everyone else. It's my world, and I no longer want you in it."

He fired two shots into LaJuan's chest, and Raine screamed, "Noooooooo!"

LaJuan fell to her knees and then face-forward to the ground. Raine broke free and ran over to her. She turned LaJuan over and caressed her, crying hysterically. Blood was oozing from the crack of LaJuan's mouth.

LaJuan grabbed Raine's shoulder, "Raine, go to the safety deposit box I left for you. There are some things in that box you need to know."

Raine said, "LaJuan, don't die on me, help is coming!"

LaJuan replied, "No Raine it's not...this is it for me...take...take care of Kim for me."

Raine was hysterical, "No, no...give your life to Christ...do it!"

LaJuan managed a smile. Raine continued, "Please, LaJuan, trust me!"

LaJuan said, "Raine, I did already..." She gently pulled Raine's head down to her and whispered something in Raine's ear. Raine was shocked. LaJuan's eyes slowly closed. Her body went limp.

Raine cried and held her tightly in her bosom, rocking back and forth. Thoughts of their relationship raced through Raine's mind. Here she was five years later, holding another sister tightly after all the life had gone out of her body.

Raine eased LaJuan's body down on the pavement. She looked back at Kek with hate. They were getting in Kek's limo. The sirens could be heard in the distance. Help was coming, but it was too late. Kek had killed another of Raine's friends and gotten away with it.

The charismatic, loving, kind Raine turned into a vengeful Raine. She was going to get revenge for her friend and her sister. These men had killed too many good people, people who were her friends and family. She had to end it. She had to rid the world of them forever.

***

Raine pulled up to the warehouse address LaJuan whispered in her ear. She walked up to the door and punched in LaJuan's birthday. It was the code she always used. She went inside.

The warehouse smelled just like it looked. This was not a place where Raine would hang out. She froze as a man approached.

"I take it she's dead."

Raine paused. Saying the words weren't easy for her, "Yes. She asked me to pick up a package from you. You're

Wayne, right?"

"You should say, 'What's your name?' By asking me if my name is Wayne, it makes it easy for me to give you the right answer. If I weren't Wayne, you wouldn't know it."

Raine nodded, "Got it."

She took the envelope from him, never looking inside, "Thanks." She turned and walked away.

"You're welcome. Be safe."

She thought, *"Safe? There's no such thing. Everywhere I go, trouble finds me."*

31

They all stood at the gravesite dressed mostly in black. Raine knew LaJuan's favorite color was black, so it fitted that she wore the best black dress she had to honor her friend. No one at the site knew LaJuan like she did. She was the closest one to her, and she would forever miss her friend. She only wished they had grown closer over the years.

Raine was asked to speak at the gravesite, and she never hesitated to accept. She stood up and took the podium. She looked at the small crowd and smiled. Raine's smile could be infectious at times. Everyone who was gathered smiled as well. She started, "Five years ago, I buried my oldest blood sister, Penny Davis. It was a sad day for the Davis family, and I will never get it out of my head."

"Today is on par with that day because although we were not related by blood, LaJuan Craig was my sister. We had differences like any family, but in the end, we both knew we loved each other. If you knew LaJuan, then you knew it wasn't easy for her to love anyone."

"Her circle was small; her friends were very few, but I know I was one of them. I held her in my arms when she took her last breath, but I was happy to hear that she had given her life to Christ before the end came. That little bit of information makes this entire process easier for me because we all must go home one day. When that day arrives and if you are right with God, then it should be like today is for LaJuan—a day filled with happiness, not pain."

"LaJuan Craig is in Heaven, rejoicing with our Lord and Savior because she asked for forgiveness of her sins, and she accepted Jesus Christ to be her Lord and Savior. Therefore, I will miss my sister greatly. I smile because I know she's in Heaven. Thank you all for being here today."

***

Raine was sitting in the car parked in front of the bank where LaJuan instructed her to get the information out of the safety deposit box. Jay, Renata, and Andra were with her. Raine left the kids and Kim with Jay's mother.

She sat in the car with her shades on, and people on the street recognized her. She didn't want to be bothered. She loved her fans very much, but this wasn't a good time for her. She was mourning the loss of her best friend and couldn't even fake a smile for the crowd.

Jay asked, "Do you want me to go inside and get the information?"

Raine didn't hear him. Her mind was focused on LaJuan and also the loss of her father. Everyone was leaving her, and in some way, it had something to do with the men in suits. She had only six months under their reign, so she didn't really know who they were, but she knew LaJuan did.

Jay asked again, "Raine, do you want me to go inside?"

Raine looked at him, "No, baby, I have to do it."

Jay replied, "Sweetheart, you know I would do anything for you." Raine didn't respond.

Raine walked into the bank and met with the bank manager. The manager guided her to the safety deposit box, checked her credentials, then left her alone to check the box.

Raine slowly opened the box. It contained a note. She read it.

> *"Raine, if you are reading this, that means I'm dead. I don't know if I decided to give my life to Christ or not, but if I didn't, well...I deserve what I get.*

You were my one and only friend. I know you hate me for the things that I did to you, and I deserve it. I can't expect you to fully understand the things that I went through in my life...no one would really understand. I'm writing you this letter with the attached documents so that you will fully know what the men in suits did to you and your family.

Several years ago, even before we met, I learned that the men in suits were a powerful organization that could affect the world we live in. They are comprised of some of the world's richest and most powerful people. They have their hands in everything, Raine!

Anyway, before I met you, they orchestrated the infection of cancer to a woman, your mother. This plan was conceived to break your family down and divide you. They knew that with your mother out of the way, your father would be too distraught to realize what was happening to his family. Then, they would send Damien Black to your church and attempt to sign your sister Penny, knowing that you would become jealous and want to sign also.

Raine, they wanted you and your soul all along. All of that was done just to sign you. What they didn't count on was the love your family had for each other. A love I admired so much that I tried to hurt you.

Your family's love was so strong that your sister sacrificed her life to save you. They didn't count on that, and that's why you were freed. The story of Job is true in your life as well because God told them that they couldn't touch you.

Raine, do not fear for me because wherever I am, you can bet that I'm good. I just ask that you find my daughter, Kim Coleman, and take care of her. The address is on one of the documents attached. I trust her with you. Take care, my one and only friend.

Love,

LaJuan Craig"

Renata was looking intently at the documents, *"These documents go back. Wow, this one is before I was born. They put this plan in motion a long time ago. They made Damien into the person he was, and if I'm reading this right, they ordered Mr. Black to kill his wife because they believed Markus would kill him and start a chain reaction that would bring Damien to them."*

All the documents were stamped with the name "The Illuminati."

Raine had so many emotions after reading the letter and documents. She burst into tears. Raine mumbled, "It's my fault, it's all my fault. Everybody died because I wanted to be a star!"

Raine gathered herself and the documents. She put the box back where it belonged and walked out of the vault. The manager met her, "Is everything okay, Mrs. Davis?"

Raine said softly, "Yes, everything is good."

She followed the manager to the door. She noticed a woman standing at a desk, filling out a slip. She was wearing shades and a hoodie. Raine stopped and stared at the woman. The woman cracked a smile and went to the teller.

The bank manager asked, "Mrs. Davis, are you okay?"

Raine turned, "Yes, thank you." She walked out of the bank and to the car where her friends were waiting.

Epilogue

Raine Davis stood in her waiting room, staring in the mirror. The family home had been destroyed by Don and his men, but her spirit wasn't broken. She had lost her mother, father, sister, and best friend. It had to end.

She planned to fight back. She looked in the mirror and said, "You may be made up of the richest and most powerful men in the world, but my God is greater than anything you got. Lord, I'm calling on you to protect my family and me as I go on this fight to expose them for who they are and what they are doing to us. They have destroyed too many lives and too many families to be allowed to continue. They destroyed my family."

Her assistant came into the room, "Ma'am, they're ready for you now."

Raine turned and smiled. She said, "Thank you," as she walked past her and out to the podium.

Her white dress and smile were enough to light the room. She looked over the room and in the very back in the shadows, she saw him. She knew he would be there. She knew he wouldn't go down without a fight, but she was ready to give him one. This young, charismatic, charming, high-spirited young lady from Florida was ready to take on the world's richest men.

"Today, I have decided to take a stance. I have decided that the world needs to know. You need to know how

in the background, the shadows to a favorable end. An end that's good for only one group of people. Today, I will take on the campaign to end this atrocity. You will no longer rule the world as you have for centuries because Raine Davis is ready to fight you or die trying."

Cameras began to flash all over the room, but Raine didn't pay attention to any of them. She focused on one man who was focused on her. This was a war between two powerful people, Raine Davis, the star who was loved by millions, and the man few knew anything about but was the most powerful man in the world.

She was determined to end the reign of the Illuminati on the world and specifically Kek's reign as the leader.

Raine smiled and looked up to the rafters. Many thought she was honoring God, but she was smiling at the person hiding in the shadows.

Her assistance leaned over, "Who's up there?"

Raine smiled, turned, and walked away.

(Read more in *Let it Raine (The Final Chapter)*.)

ABOUT THE AUTHOR

Gerald C. Anderson, Sr. was born and raised in Tampa, Florida. He spent most of his childhood life growing up in the Belmont Heights area of Tampa.

In 1980, Gerald graduated from C. Leon King Senior High School in Temple Terrace, Florida. Following graduation he enlisted in the United States Air Force.

Air Force Life

In his service career Gerald traveled the world with assignments to California (twice), Florida, Kansas, Maryland, West Germany, and Korea. Upon his last assignment in Maryland and after retirement from the Air Force, Gerald began working in the United States Federal Government's Department of Energy. In 2003, he moved to the Internal Revenue Service and in 2007 he joined the Department of Education.

Education

In 2005, Gerald obtained his Bachelors of Science degree in Computer Information Systems from Strayer University and in 2008 he obtained his Masters of Administration degree in Criminal Justice Administration from the University of Cincinnati (UC).

Published Books

Following his graduation from UC Gerald wrote his first book, entitled, "We Come In Peace". Not wanting to stop there, Gerald released his second book, "27 Hours (What Would You Do If You Faced The End?" through his own publishing company, Gerald C. Anderson Publishing and it is currently available through Amazon. Gerald's third and most successful book, "Standing Firm (One Family's Fight Against Domestic Violence)" was released in May of 2015. November of 2016 brought Gerald's fourth book entitled, "Secrets (Silent Scream In The Dark)".

Righteous Productions and The Lyfe Magazine

In August of 2015, Gerald and Renata M. Smith agreed to become business partners and started Righteous Productions. Together they wrote the script for the movie version of Standing Firm and co-produced the movie.

In late 2016, Righteous Productions launched the successful magazine, "The Lyfe Magazine". The Lyfe Magazine is a Christian lifestyle magazine with a mission to inform, educate and entertain people.

A Saved Man

In 1992, Gerald turned his life over to Jesus Christ and a life with Christ at the head. He is currently a musician in church. He continues to reside in Maryland with his son.

SAVED

www.ingramcontent.com/pod-product-compliance
Lightning Source LLC
Chambersburg PA
CBHW060919040426
42445CB00011B/692